The Construction of Minority Identities
in France and Britain

The Construction of Minority Identities in France and Britain

Edited by

Gino G. Raymond
Professor of Modern French Studies,
University of Bristol, UK

and

Tariq Modood
Professor of Sociology,
Politics and Public Policy,
University of Bristol, UK

First published in 2007 by
PALGRAVE MACMILLAN
Houndmills, Basingstoke, Hampshire RG21 6XS and
175 Fifth Avenue, New York, N.Y. 10010
Companies and representatives throughout the world.

PALGRAVE MACMILLAN is the global academic imprint of the Palgrave
Macmillan division of St. Martin's Press, LLC and of Palgrave Macmillan Ltd.
Macmillan® is a registered trademark in the United States, United Kingdom
and other countries. Palgrave is a registered trademark in the European
Union and other countries.

ISBN-13: 978–0–230–52218–3 hardback
ISBN-10: 0–230–52218–1 hardback

This book is printed on paper suitable for recycling and made from fully
managed and sustained forest sources. Logging, pulping and manufacturing
processes are expected to conform to the environmental regulations of
the country of origin.

A catalogue record for this book is available from the British Library.

Library of Congress Cataloging-in-Publication Data

   The construction of minority identities in France and Britain / edited by
Gino G. Raymond and Tariq Modood.
      p. cm.
   Includes bibliographical references and index.
   ISBN 0–230–52218–1 (alk. paper)
      1. Minorities – France. 2. Minorities – Great Britain. 3. Muslims –
France. 4. Muslims – Great Britain. 5. France – Ethnic relations. 6. Great
Britain – Ethnic relations. I. Raymond, Gino. II. Modood, Tariq.

DC34.C612 2007
305.800941—dc22   2007023311

10   9   8   7   6   5   4   3   2   1
16 15 14 13 12 11 10 09 08 07

Printed and bound in Great Britain by
Antony Rowe Ltd, Chippenham and Eastbourne

Contents

Acknowledgements

This project is the fruit of a unique collaboration between leading academics in France and Britain, who shared their knowledge at a conference organised by the Departments of French and of Sociology at the University of Bristol in the autumn of 2004 with the aim of launching a cross-Channel debate on the construction of minority identities. The editors would like to express their gratitude to the Institut Français, the Leverhulme Trust and the University of Bristol, without whose generous material and moral support the original event and the publications it has engendered would not have been possible.

Notes on the Contributors

Harry Goulbourne is Professor of Sociology at the South Bank University in London. As well as being a frequent commentator in the media, he is the author of major recent studies such as *Race Relations in Britain since 1945* (1998) and editor of *Race and Ethnicity* (2001).

Riva Kastoryano is a Professor at the Institut d'Études Politiques and trained as an economist as well as a sociologist. She taught at Harvard before taking up her post in Paris. Her major publications include *Les codes de la différence* (2005, editor), and *Negotiating Identities. States and Immigrants in France and Germany* (2002).

Nadia Kiwan possesses both a British PhD and a French doctorate from the Ecole des Hautes Études in Paris. She is currently lecturing at the University of Aberdeen and is the author of a major forthcoming study entitled *Identities, Discourses and Experiences: Young People of North African Origin in France* (2007). She has also contributed to a number of edited works on race, identity and citizenship.

Vincent Latour is Maître de conférences at the Université de Toulouse and a member of a CNRS team researching issues of identity in Europe. He is the author of *Les relations raciales en Grande-Bretagne: le cas de la communauté indo-pakistanaise de Bristol* (2005) and has written a number of articles on race and identity in popular journals such as *Alternatives Internationales*.

Tariq Modood, OBE, is Professor of Sociology, Politics and Public Policy at the University of Bristol. He is Director of the Leverhulme Programme on Migration and Citizenship and his most recent monograph is entitled *Multicultural Politics: Racism, Ethnicity and Muslims in Europe* (2005).

Gino G. Raymond is Professor of Modern French Studies at the University of Bristol and has published widely on French culture and politics. His recent books include *The French Communist Party under the Fifth Republic* (2005) and *Redefining the French Republic* (2006, editor with A. Cole).

Max Silverman is Professor of Modern French Studies at the University of Leeds. He is the author of the seminal work, *Deconstructing the Nation: Immigration, Racism and Citizenship in Modern France* (1992). His other books reflect his interest in the intellectual culture of France and include

Facing Postmodernity: Contemporary French Thought on Culture and Society (1999).

Pnina Werbner is Professor of Social Anthropology at the University of Keele and an expert in migrations, community formation and the role of women. Her recent books include: *The Migration Process* (2002); *Imagined Diasporas among Manchester Muslims* (2002); and *Pilgrims of Love: the Anthropology of a Global Sufi Cult* (2003). She is the co-editor of the *Postcolonial Encounters* series published by Zed Books.

Michel Wieviorka is a Professor at the École des Hautes Études en Sciences Sociales in Paris and one of France's leading sociologists. He has authored over 20 books covering areas such as racism, multiculturalism and social movements. Recent titles include: *The Arena of Racism* (1995); *La différence* (2005) and *La tentation anti-sémite* (2006). He is also editor of the monthly magazine, *Le Monde des Débats*.

Catherine Wihtol de Wenden is a Professor at the Institut d'Études Politiques in Paris and has spent the past two decades studying international migrations and the challenges they pose. She has been an adviser on these matters to the OECD, the European Commission and the UNHCR. Her recent books include *L'Europe des migrations* (2001) and *Atlas des migrations dans le monde* (2005).

Introduction

Gino G. Raymond and Tariq Modood

When, on Saturday 22 October 2005, violence erupted between the black and Asian communities of the Lozells district of Birmingham, it appeared to confirm the views of a number of French commentators about the manner in which minorities in Britain were managed, or, more precisely, not managed with regard to their integration into the national community. Although some uncertainty hovered over the direct cause of the dispute that sparked off the riot that night, it was generally acknowledged that tension had been simmering between the two communities for some time, perhaps even years. Viewed from across the Channel, the familiar response was to view this event as another example of the possible consequences of the British predilection for *enfermement* rather than an unequivocal policy of integration, the downside of a supposedly flexible policy of allowing communities to construct a separate social identity that expresses the distinctness of their culture, but that in reality 'encloses' or isolates them. This French response appeared to be justified by the intervention of Lord Ouseley, a former head of the Commission for Racial Equality, when he accused the CRE under its new leadership of having spent too much time focusing on the 'soft' cultural issues such as the terminology of the race debate, rather than the harder issues lying at the root of the grievances of residents in places like Lozells.

Conversely, the much more damaging riots that occurred nightly for weeks on end during November 2005 in the ring of deprived suburbs around Paris and that were emulated in provincial towns as far apart as Toulouse and Strasbourg, drew a familiar response from British shores. In many Anglo-Saxon eyes they were testament to an overly inflexible French policy of assimilating communities into 'la République, une et indivisible', that is a unitary national identity that by definition cannot be subdivided into distinct communitarian parts. As the leader in *The Guardian* of 8 November argued, the country which had had so little time in the past for the British approach to multiculturalism, now had to face the incontrovertible evidence of the need for some kind of policy resembling the British one of community cohesion. In other words, preserving and celebrating the diversity of its cultural communities as the best way of counteracting the incipient sense of discrimination that can ultimately lead to social conflict.

The originality of this volume is the way it brings together these characteristic, even stereotypical responses, and elucidates the common challenges the two societies face. Both contend with the legacies of an imperial past and more particularly the dramatic change wrought by the arrival of substantial numbers of non-white immigrants, drawn into communities often distinguished from their host community and from each other by a strong and separate sense of identity. Drawing on expert contributions that cut across cultural studies and the social sciences, this volume provides fresh insights into how, for example, the apparently universalist rigidities of the French republican approach to minorities sometimes conceal a surprising willingness on the part of the state to concede the right to a separate sense of identity in the bargaining that occurs at local level. Conversely, other contributions go against the grain of received wisdom concerning Britain, arguing that there are unifying assumptions that underlie the apparently piecemeal pragmatism of the British approach, such as the increasing reliance on economic initiatives at grass-roots level to counteract the disadvantages generated by the inequalities that may be ascribed to racial and/or cultural identity. The first part of this study therefore analyses the characteristics and contradictions of French and British approaches to the understanding of how minority identities are constructed. Then, from the realm of conjecture and theoretical speculation, the study moves to the realities on the ground, with regard to more recently established and older minorities with distinct identities in both France and Britain.

On one level therefore, the Franco-British comparison is based on an obvious point of departure. The ideological underpinning of the French Republic still conforms, in essence, to the voluntarist convictions articulated by Jules Ferry at the end of the nineteenth century, that it was the mission of the Jacobin state to forge, through its operation in the public sphere and especially the education system, a uniform adherence to the secular credo of the Republic. The celebration, in 2007, of the tercentenary of the Act of Union between England and Scotland, and the devolution of power to the constituent parts of the United Kingdom that has occurred since the beginning of the twenty-first century, illustrate the way the British unitary state has evolved by accretion and the general pragmatism that has marked the management of that unity into the present. Consequently, while it may be argued that there are more logical comparisons in terms of policy, cultural assumptions and outcomes (such as Britain and the Netherlands or France and Germany), we contend that it is the opposite and fundamental assumptions shaping the British and French polities that make the way they address the manner in which minorities construct their identities within their midst uniquely fascinating, and indicative of national processes of self-understanding.

But the overarching virtue of stretching the argument between these two poles is that it facilitates the weaving, through the variety of contributions to this volume, of complex evocations of how the very idea of identity and the processes of self-identification develop, change and even defy the attempt to impose interpretative frameworks that weight the understanding of that change in one ideological direction or another. With hindsight, the factor of race in the construction of identity was a relatively straightforward vector whose movement could be tracked, along with the opposition between minority communities and established majority populations. The emergence of religion as a factor cutting across these considerations has added a major layer of complexity, and as some of the grassroots research in this volume reveals, the very construction of a sense of identity is now refracted through processes of 'subjectivisation' that make the resulting sense of being far from fixed or predictable.

The first part of this volume adumbrates approaches to an understanding of the construction of minority identities. In 'Secularism and the Accommodation of Muslim Identities', Tariq Modood and Riva Kastoryano develop a broad view of the assumptions at the heart of secularism in countries like France, Britain and Western societies in general. The fundamental given in the foregoing states is the distinction between the public and the private realm. But if we look at the countries of Europe more closely, for example, we see that secularism takes various shapes, according to national cultures, traditions and experiences such as, crucially, nation-building. This process is not without its contradictions, as illustrated by a country like Britain which has an established church in the Church of England yet is a society that, according to commonly recognised criteria, is one of the most secular in Europe. Conversely, the European republic most consciously committed to expelling the influence of religion from the public realm also set about consecrating the ideals of Jacobin republicanism in profoundly religious terms, from the cult of the Supreme Being to the state-sponsored processions venerating the symbolic representations of French republican virtues such as reason and liberty.

Once the paradox implicit in the creation of a secular 'faith' has been digested, it is evident that what sets France apart from Anglo-American liberal democracies is that the secular polity is not the result of the separation of Church and state. Rather, in France the Republic is the agent of change to this effect, instead of being an impartial arbiter. The French state's attempt to regularise the position of Islam and its followers in France, through the official recognition given to the Conseil Français du Culte Musulman (Muslim Council of France), follows the pattern established for the institutionalisation of Catholics, Protestants and Jews. The purpose of this institutional embrace on the part of the Republic is to educate the citizen to recognise the primacy of the values of the Republic in the public sphere, while enjoying the freedom to identify him or herself as a believer, with the accompanying cultural markers, in the private sphere. But as the authors argue, the distinctions between public and private, political and cultural, are far from clear or fixed. Moreover, the political culture of a polity may purport to express an abstract neutrality, but in reality it has absorbed the values, religious and cultural, of the people over whom, over time, it has deployed its institutional emanations. The consequence for the newly settled communities in the state, therefore, and most obviously the Muslim community, is that the rhetoric of secular neutrality by the state can be read as a pretext for a partiality that militates against genuine pluralism and multiculturalism. Established political discourse thus fails to respond to the growing need for a new understanding of equality that plucks it out of the abstract and reinterprets it as a valorisation of difference that operates in both the public and the private spheres: a politics of recognition. As Modood and Kastoryano concede, however, the process of institutionalising recognition is where the cultures of Britain and France may diverge the most.

'The Construction of What?' is an appropriately provocative title for Michel Wieviorka's overview of the way the understanding of identity and the processes of its construction have evolved, the paradoxes this evolution has generated and the challenges it now poses. Beginning with the assumption commonly held in the 1960s that the demand for the recognition of cultural identities in the public sphere might simply be due to reproduction, namely the instinctive need to regenerate an inherited identity rooted in time immemorial, Wieviorka traces the shift to the dominant belief in the 1990s that identities were invented, even cobbled together. Concomitant with this shift was a more problematic understanding of individualism, or the contradictory pulls to which it was subject: on the one hand there was the pull of the public sphere that required the deployment of reason and the acknowledgement of constitutional and legal constraints if the individual was to assume his or her citizenship; on the other hand there was the less rational pull exercised by the affinity with group identities, convictions and traditions. An additional layer of complexity was added by the confusion that sometimes arose concerning whether demands for the recognition of identity were truly cultural in origin, or in fact socioeconomic, such as the disadvantages endured in the housing and jobs market. Notwithstanding this confusion, however, Wieviorka acknowledges that there is a dynamic relationship between the cultural and the social, in that it is difficult to understand the cultural demands of individuals or groups without a grasp of the social conditions they inhabit.

In 'Debating Cultural Difference in France', Catherine Wihtol de Wenden offers a broad, historical view of the factors that have shaped modern France and conditioned the peculiarities and paradoxes of the French attitude to the construction of minority identities. The revolution of 1789 was in many ways a struggle against the cultural and linguistic identities that divided France at regional level. Crucial to the pursuit of a unified state was the creation of a citizen, characterised by the values he shared with fellow citizens rather than the communitarian loyalties that might set him apart. This was a long-term project and, de Wenden argues, the ethno-cultural concomitant of the unified state, i.e. the homogeneous nation, did not flower fully in ideological terms until the Third Republic, and especially in response to the disastrous consequences for France of the Franco-Prussian War.

The pressure to recognise and valorise regional identities did not of course disappear, sometimes taking nostalgic literary or linguistic forms. But it was under the Vichy regime that a systematic attempt was made to privilege regional cultures, in opposition to the template of unity provided by the Republic. The association of such a project with Vichy did much to discredit it, but it is arguable that half a century later, due to the pressures of globalisation, there are greater numbers of French people willing to seek refuge in local and regional socio-economic networks and what they regard as a more secure sense of identity. Moreover, the process of decentralisation that began in the 1980s has led to paradoxical situations where the unified French state appears to give with one hand and withhold with the other. For example, recognising the right of Corsicans and Bretons to teach their language in state-funded schools, but withholding recognition of them as 'peoples'. Undeniably, however, the most complex twists to these paradoxes have resulted from mass immigration to France from its former colonies. While, on the one hand, the pressure from the success of the extreme right at the polls pushed the political class as a whole to accentuate the need to revive belief in those universalist values that are meant to yoke citizens equally to a collective social project, on the other hand the undeniable needs of specific communities have resulted in the de facto adoption of very un-French measures such as positive discrimination. One might argue therefore that the peculiarity of the multicultural reality of the French Republic is to be found in a process of continuous bargaining between a historically uniformising state, and minorities whose identities and loyalties are increasingly pluralised.

In 'The French Republic Unveiled', Max Silverman focuses on the ambiguities, and what some might regard as the absurdities, revealed by the attempt of the French state to police the secular boundaries of the public space in the Republic. Paradoxically, it may well be argued that the more homogenising states insist on suppressing what they regard as threats to the neutrality of the public sphere, the more they highlight the differences they wish to eliminate. Searching for the intellectual roots of this posture in France, Silverman identifies what he regards as the false universalism of the Enlightenment, positing a view of 'Man' that lacked the self-consciousness to recognise the culture- and gender-specific context from which it emerged. The subsequent development of republican culture in France and the correspondingly immutable symbols of its identity have conditioned a response to symbolic markers that often misread the way they are used in a postmodern society. Rather than reflecting any monolithic political motives, the choice to wear a headscarf or engage in a particular cultural practice may be part of a shifting and highly individualised form of self-definition in an age of increasing rootlessness.

While the consequences and particularly the constraints imposed by the demands of faith-based forms of identification in certain communities, especially for women, are not to be underestimated, it is legitimate to question whether they do not in fact serve to occlude fault-lines that are more economic than social. The less states can do to influence the play of global economic forces, the more they may compensate for this by ostentatiously policing boundaries, such as that between the public and the private spheres, especially in a country like France, where the republican state possesses such a long historical mission to forge a common national culture. However, Silverman's criticism extends to Britain too, where the failure to respond constructively to the demands for an empowering form of recognition is often due to a rigidly antithetical form of thinking characterised by old boundaries that can no longer contain the 'deterritorialised' and hybridised identities of today.

In the second part of this volume attention shifts to how the construction of minority identities is experienced by those concerned. In 'Shifting Sociocultural Identities: Young People of North African Origin in France', Nadia Kiwan describes the research undertaken at grassroots level in urban France, over a 12-month period between 2000 and 2001 in Aubervilliers, a town on the periphery of Paris. At the heart of her research lay a series of interviews with 64 young people of North African background, aged between 16 and 31. Surveys of academic and media analysis of this particular group by Kiwan revealed intellectual discourses shaped by two principal ideological oppositions: on the one hand, the antithesis between universalism and particularism, where the individual citizen is opposed to the community; and on the other hand, an almost exclusive focus on socio-economic factors determining the nature of life in the *banlieues* that pays unacceptably scant regard to the reality that the landscape in question is largely inhabited by large populations of immigrant origin.

The originality of Kiwan's analysis lies in her attempt to constitute an approach that is both social and cultural to the understanding of the problematic of integration and identification represented by immigrant and post-migrant populations in France. The fruits of Kiwan's research among her sample group of young people defy the familiar ideological paradigms that have attempted to characterise the construction of identity. In a finding that may well resonate with the experiences of other groups from different origins outside France, Kiwan's interviews with her respondents paint a picture of young individuals tailoring a sense of self that is the result of continuously circulating between social and cultural forms of identification, while simultaneously drawing on community-oriented and more universal elements of identity.

In 'Converging at Last? France, Britain and their Minorities', Vincent Latour draws on the research among black and minority ethnic groups in Bristol, which he has been conducting over most of the past decade, to reflect on the different trajectories taken by race relations in Britain and France and to explore the convergences in policy terms between the two countries. Notwithstanding the familiar French perception of the British approach to race relations as community-based, and therefore divisive in national terms, and the classic British perception of the French attitude as oppressively assimilationist, both countries have had to confront the shortcomings in their attitudes to their minorities in the light of the persistent tensions that have surfaced in recent years, and even tacitly concede that they have something to learn from each other.

As Latour's research in Bristol illustrates, there is evidence to suggest that the community-based British approach to race relations offers little scope for complacency in terms of tangible results, vis-à-vis the French approach. Across a range of criteria including employment and education, it is clear that the gap between some sections of the ethnic minorities and the white population is widening. Moreover, it may be argued that the community-based approach may allow for a kind of self-segregation and isolation. As Latour discovers in inner-city Bristol, supposedly non-confessional voluntary organisations operating at the community level can, in reality, fragment along ethnic and religious lines and, for example, instead of serving the needs of the 'Asian' community, follow traditional fault-lines between 'Sikh', 'Hindu' and 'Muslim'. Some of the policy responses to such challenges at government level, such as the pursuit of 'community cohesion', the creation of citizenship ceremonies and the introduction of citizenship education, suggest that the French state's emphasis on integration into a national community may not be wholly inappropriate to Britain. On the other hand, while a radical conversion in France to the Anglo-Saxon investment in communities as the way to better race relations is unlikely, there are signs of the acceptance of multiracial difference and the concomitant diversity of identities as factors in the formulation of policy. Thus the secular French state school system has accepted the need to teach its pupils about world religions, and the officially neutral state has given its support to a Conseil Français du Culte Musulman, in a move reminiscent of the pragmatism more typical of the British approach.

'Veiled Interventions in Pure Space: Honour, Shame and Embodied Struggles among Muslims in Britain and France', allows Pnina Werbner to adopt an approach that is both very broad and very specific. She begins with a broad overview of the cultural dynamics generated by international migration, and in particular the way issues such as honour and shame have found symbolic significance in the dress codes of young women in a way that crosses frontiers, connecting value systems and cultures of origin with the new cultures in which migrant communities find themselves. Werbner brings out the variety and complexity that characterise the operation of notions like honour and shame in

Muslim communities, and the tendency of secular Western societies to envisage them in rather reductive terms. Moreover, she evokes the way these issues relate to the institution of marriage and the intergenerational tension that can result as parents of British-born Asians sometimes 'instrumentalise' the tradition of arranged marriage with a partner from the subcontinent as a means of underwriting family honour and distancing the prospect of choices by their offspring that might incur shame.

Drawing specifically on Michel Foucault's theoretical contribution to the understanding of human sexuality, Werbner argues that the symbolic representation of female sexuality has meshed with the narrative of modernity that is so central to the self-understanding of modern France and republican values, and led to some profound contradictions. So that, for example, while the process of veiling may be perceived by the advocates of secularism as symptomatic of a value system that sets its face against modernity by denying individuals their rights because of their gender, those same critics of the veil will confuse sexual licence with modernity and fail to address the gender-based discrimination and degradation practised in the ubiquitous rise of pornography. More disturbingly still, Werbner suggests that the defence of the secular nature of the public sphere in France rings hollow given the lessons of history, when it was precisely the most invisible minority, that had most successfully adapted to the ideology of the Republic, that was most ferociously persecuted during the Second World War, i.e. the Jews.

Finally, in 'The Construction of Identity, Integration and Participation of Caribbeans in British Society', Harry Goulbourne discusses an earlier wave of migrants who have been missing from view so far, but whose arrival as the first post-war wave of migrants to the UK played a crucial role in launching the debate on immigration and identity. The designation 'Caribbeans' covers a rich diversity of identities relating to the different islands in the region, reflecting the varied histories of European conquest and non-European settlement. While post-colonial nation-building, and the emergence of unifying sporting and literary achievements helped shape a recognisable West Indian personality, the arrival in Britain and the new contexts in which Caribbeans had to operate were instrumental in engendering a collective identity.

The uniqueness of the Caribbean experience lies in the fact that, in sociopolitical terms, their integration into British life has succeeded arguably to the point of virtual absorption. The cultural proximity to the majority indigenous population was grounded in shared language, religion, customs and traditions. Notwithstanding the racially motivated intolerance encountered by the Caribbeans who began to arrive in large numbers in the UK in the immediate post-war period, the post-Columbian societies created under British rule in their islands of origin had fostered a hybridity that was highly adaptable to life in their new home. The emergence of a 'creole' society in the Caribbean, for instance, had conditioned the willingness of Caribbeans to enter into interracial and interethnic social relationships. As Goulbourne argues, there is no other new minority group in British society that is more socially intertwined with the indigenous population, especially at the base of the social pyramid. With regard to cultural assimilation, there is no other minority whose contribution, for example, to sport, music or popular entertainment has so readily become grafted onto indigenous forms of practice or production, whether it is white reggae bands or urban carnival. The campaigns led by Carribeans against discrimination, such as the use of the 'sus' laws by police forces, have been characterised by the fact that the goal was to improve the condition of wider society, not only their own community. While the motivation for this may have been a pragmatic recognition of the need to gather broad support, it may nonetheless contain a lesson for other minority communities.

As the findings of the Policy Exchange think tank study released in early 2007 suggest, the younger generation of Muslims in Britain feel they have less in common with their non-Muslim fellow-citizens than their parents do. Notwithstanding the possible margin for error in the sampling, it is fair to assume that the British policy of community cohesion has yet to deliver the results hoped for. Even after the assurances given by the governing elite following the events of autumn 2005 in France, the truth remains that in any given week in urban areas, vehicles will be torched by disaffected youths, largely from the ethnic minorities, as a direct challenge to the authority of the host society that has failed to integrate them. The essays in this volume therefore provide a timely reflection on the challenges facing France and Britain as they endeavour to respond to the subjective needs of all their citizens, in an increasingly globalised world.

Part I

Approaches to an Understanding of the Construction of Minority Identities

1

Secularism and the Accommodation of Muslim Identities[1]

Tariq Modood and Riva Kastoryano

Introduction

Secularism has long been regarded as a settled, non-controversial feature of Western societies. While a century or more of intra-Christian wars more or less gave way to the principle agreed in the Treaty of Westphalia of 1648, *Cujus regio, ejus religio* ('The religion of the prince is the religion of the people'), namely that the religion of the ruler was to be the religion of the state/country,[2] this principle was subsequently chipped away at. Not only did toleration come to be seen as equally important but the Enlightenment of the eighteenth century in various ways challenged the Christian faith, the authority of the Church, and the promotion of a religion by the state. With the militant example of the French Revolution, the secularist anti-Westphalian principle of the separation of Church and state, of religion and politics, has progressively become hegemonic. By the middle of the twentieth century it was universally taken for granted in Western societies (one of the few principles that was shared by liberalism, socialism and most versions of nationalism) and thought to be one of the defining features of modernity. Moreover, the Westphalian prioritising of territorial allegiance over doctrinal truth and allegiance to a community of co-believers has been triumphant in the politics of Western societies. It has not been entirely without its challengers but the challengers have been forms of secular internationalism such as socialism or cosmopolitanism, rather than religious communities or movements.

Yet in the founding countries of secularism, the principle and its interpretation in specific contexts have gradually been challenged on the grounds of religion in the last 20, and especially in the last 10, years. This challenge, especially in Western Europe, has been associated with the demand of some newly settled Muslim peoples to seek institutional expression for their Muslim identity. Muslims today are citizens or long-term residents in many Western countries and are demanding institutional representation and recognition within these national societies. As Muslims are outside the long relationship between state and Church that made Western national histories, they do not always see the historical compromises of the relationships applied to their demands. Related to this is the fact that Muslims do not sometimes appreciate the stresses and compromises of that history and why their demands are sometimes met with exasperation, even by some of their political allies. Nevertheless, Muslim claims for religious recognition in one form or another are central to multicultural debates. The truly democratic response to this unexpected development requires that the principles and the institutional and juridical arrangements of secularism must be revisited.

Varieties of secular states

At the heart of secularism is a distinction between the public realm of citizens and policies, and the private realm of belief and worship. While all European Union countries are clearly secular in many ways, interpretations and the institutional arrangements diverge according to the dominant national religious culture and the differing projects of nation-state building and thus make secularism a 'particular' experience. This also applies to different forms of Enlightenment rationalism. In Germany the Enlightenment philosophy (*Aufklärung*) was not really against religion as in France, just as rationality was not against Protestant piety. The concern for equality it embodied consisted mainly of destroying the barriers between the clergy, the nobility, the middle class and the peasantry.[3] After the formation of the German state, the *Kulturkampf* was, as in France, characterised by an effort to guarantee social cohesion by minimising the role of the Catholic Church while limiting Protestant influence on politics as well. Yet in Germany, the religious freedoms granted to Catholics and Lutherans assumed a corporative nature, 'granting equal rights only to communities formed as corporations', recognised by the public law.[4] This can be seen in the West German (FDR) social democratic model, in which (while the most formidable social partners in governance were industrialists and trade unions), the churches too had a corporatist place, with the state collecting funds for them (voluntary taxes) and paying for denominational teaching in schools out of general taxes. The churches have also been important political actors at various times. For example, some Protestant churches were active in the protest movements that led to the tearing down of the Berlin Wall in 1989.

British Enlightenment philosophers like David Hume were sceptical about the supernaturalistic claims of religion, which they felt should be subject to the claims of empirical science, but were not hostile to religion as such, which they thought had useful social functions such as a practical vehicle for the acquisition of morality. Moreover, the monarchical church in Britain, the Church of England, had much less social or political power than the Catholic Church in some countries. Hence there was no reason for a radical attack on the role of the established church in Britain. In other countries, whether within the Catholic sphere, such as Ireland and Poland, or outside it as in the case of Denmark and Greece, the national church was a source of resistance against an occupying power and so played a political role that was welcomed by many nationals and which too meant that radical secularism lacked support in those countries and few castigated the Church as anti-Enlightenment. Hence, there are a number of churches within the European Union states that have or recently had, formally or informally, a national political role. Of course that does not mean that they are not secular states. It means that countries such as England, Denmark and Greece believe that secularism is compatible with having state or 'established' churches. These and other states, such as the Netherlands and Germany, extensively support denominational schools, or denominational worship and lessons in schools, out of public funds. This is not because these societies are more religious than France or other members of the European Union. In England, there is an established church, about a quarter of all school pupils are taught in state-funded religious schools and yet England is one of most secular societies in Europe, measured in terms of worship, personal religious affiliation and theistic belief.[5] The case of England suggests a distinction between state and societies which can be used further to illustrate that secularism can take different, even contradictory, forms in contemporary, liberal democratic societies.

On the other side of the Atlantic, the American Constitution emphasises the 'protection of religious diversity as a value'.[6] The United States has as its First Amendment to the Constitution that there shall be no established church and there is wide support for this; in the last few decades there has been a tendency among academics and jurists to interpret the Church–state separation in continually more radical ways.[7]

Yet, as is well known, not only is the US a deeply religious society, with much higher levels of church attendance than in Western Europe,[8] but there is a strong Protestant, evangelical fundamentalism that is rare in Europe. This fundamentalism does not necessarily dispute the 'no establishment clause' in the Constitution but is one of the primary mobilising forces in American politics and it is widely claimed that it decided the presidential election of 2004. The churches in question (mainly white, mainly in the South and Midwest) campaign openly for candidates and parties, indeed raise large sums of money for politicians and introduce religion-based issues into politics, such as positions on abortion, HIV/Aids, homosexuality, stem-cell research, prayer at school and so on. It has been said that no openly avowed atheist has ever been a candidate for the White House and that it would be impossible for such a candidate to be elected. It is not at all unusual for politicians (in fact, for President George W. Bush, it is most usual) to talk publicly about their faith, to appeal to religion and to hold prayer meetings in government buildings. On the other hand, in establishment Britain, bishops sit in the upper chamber of the legislature by right and only the senior archbishop can crown a new head of state, the monarch, but politicians rarely talk about their religion. It was noticeable, for example, that when Prime Minister Blair went to a summit meeting with President Bush to discuss aspects of the Iraq War in 2003, the US media widely reported that the two leaders had prayed together. Yet, Prime Minister Blair, one of the most openly professed and active Christians ever to hold that office, refused to answer questions on this issue from the British media on his return, saying it was a private matter. The British state may have an established church but the beliefs of the Queen's first minister are his own concern.

France draws the distinction between state and religion differently again. Like the US, there is no state church but unlike the US, the state actively promotes the privatisation of religion. While in the US, organised religion in civil society is powerful and seeks to exert influence on the political process, French civil society does not carry signs or expressions of religion. Although the transition to the Republic and to secularism swept away religion from the public space, paradoxically it maintained a religious vocabulary to express the sacred character of the Republic. This is partly a reflection of historical debates about whether a public order is possible without the support that religion gives to the promotion of moral virtues such as truth-telling and fellow-feeling for others. It has, for example, led moralists like Rousseau to argue that a public order must take over one of the traditional functions of religion, the production of social virtues and responsible conduct, and so must go beyond legislation and law enforcement and seek to produce virtuous citizens. As a matter of fact the Republic, called 'the oldest daughter of the Church', has for some a holy character. Claude Nicolet has pointed to the religious metaphors used in the establishment of moral rules and of how the Republic has been described as an Enlightenment Church.[9] Even Renan, in his famous lecture on the nation, spoke of 'the Jacobin Church' and defined it as a secular religion. When the republicans (secularists) defeated the anti-republicans (defenders of religion in public life) the representatives of the Church became civil servants, exercising certain functions allowed by the state, sometimes on behalf of the state. The state confers institutional legal status on the Catholic clergy, the Protestants of the National Federation of the Protestant Churches of France, and to the Jews governed by the Consistory created under Napoleon. Yet all references to religion disappeared from the public arena: its symbols, for example, were removed from the walls of public welfare hospitals. Public vocabulary also was secularised by using the adjective 'civil' in expressing the fundamental bonds in society: 'civil order', 'civil state', 'civil right', 'civil marriage', 'civil burial'. Thus, 'civil' replaced the holy.[10] While the Constitution of 1795 introduced such a secularisation of marriage, health and education, the full legal separation of Church and state dates from only 1905, after the Dreyfus Affair revealed extensive anti-Semitism among officials and soldiers of the state. Belief in God was now only a private matter. Even then it was not until the Constitution of 1946 that secularism became law, and that was reiterated in the Constitution of 1958, with Article 2 declaring: 'France is an indivisible, secular (*laïque*), democratic, and social Republic. It insures equality to all of its citizens before the law without distinction of origin, race and religion. It respects all beliefs.'

In this article France is not necessarily different from the American Constitution. What is different between these two countries is the organisation of religious diversity: the place of religion in civil society and its relationship to the state, the interpretation (not its juridical definition) of the principle of separation of Church and state. In France, a republican state does not just separate itself from civil society but it leads civil society by creating a political culture that is opposed to clericalism, or perhaps even to 'Catholic culture' (*esprit*). For the French Republic, *laïcité* is considered an active movement from a community ruled by the Church to a society ruled by law, and thus integral to modernity. Emancipation, the political goal consequent upon the Enlightenment, is seen as extracting the individual from religious constraints and integrating him into the political community as an individual citizen. The secular state is not so much a product but the agent of this movement. The disappearance of the sacred, which for Weber characterised modernity, means a new structure of power replaces the religious community by a political community that is allegedly the only one necessary for modernity and that has political legitimacy because it is universal.

Therefore, what distinguishes France from the United States is not a fundamental juridical or constitutional principle, but rather the role of the state in civil society. While in the United States, organised religion in civil society is powerful and seeks to exert influence on the political process, the French state promotes secularism in civil society, through representative religious institutions and programmes of education.

What are the appropriate limits of the state in relation to religion? Everyone will agree that there should be religious freedom and that this should include freedom of belief and worship in private associations. Family too falls on the private side of the line, but the state regulates the limits of what is a lawful family (for example, polygamy is not permitted in many countries), not to mention the deployment of official definitions of family in the distribution of welfare entitlements. Turning to the third item on the list, religions typically put a premium on mutuality and on care of the sick, the homeless, the elderly and so on. They set up organisations to pursue these aims, but so do states. Should there be a competitive or a cooperative relationship between these religious and state organisations, or do they have to ignore each other? Can public money (raised out of taxes on religious as well as non-religious citizens) not be used to support the organisations favoured by some religious taxpayers? What of schools? Do parents not have the right to expect that schools will make an effort (while pursuing broader educational and civic aims) not to create a conflict between the work of the school and the upbringing of the children at home but, rather, show respect for their religious background? Can parents, as associations of religious citizens, not set up their own schools and should those schools not be supported out of the taxes of the same parents? Is the school where the private, the family meets the public, the state; or is it, in some Platonic manner, where the state takes over the children from the family and pursues its own purposes? Even if there is to be no established church, the state may still wish to work with organised religion as a social partner, as is the case in Germany, or to have some forum in which it consults with organised religion, some kind of national council of religions, as in Belgium. Or, even if it does not do that because it is regarded as compromising the principle of secularism, political parties, being agents in civil society rather than organs of the state, may wish to do this and institute special representation for religious groups as many do for groups defined by age, gender, region, language, ethnicity and so on. It is clear then that the 'public' is a multifaceted concept and in relation to secularism may be defined differently in relation to different dimensions of religion and in different countries.

We can all be secularists then, all approve of secularism in some respect, and yet have quite different ideas, influenced by historical legacies and varying pragmatic compromises, of where to draw the line between public and private. It would be quite mistaken to suppose that all religious spokespersons, or at least all political Muslims, are on one side of the line, and all others are on the other side. There are many different ways of drawing the various lines at issue. In the past, the drawing of these lines has reflected particular contexts shaped by differential customs, urgency of need and awareness of the sensibilities of the relevant religious groups.[11] Exactly the same considerations are relevant in relation to the accommodation of Muslims in Europe today; not a battle of slogans and ideological oversimplifications.

The 'universality' of secularism lies in the principle of equality according to which there is no domination of one religion (the majority, therefore the national) over other religions in a de facto minority situation. Hence the assumption of state neutrality in respect of religion: the state does not have a view about any of the religions in society but ensures the freedom of individuals to practise (or not) their religion. Yet today, the private/public distinction, the ideas of state neutrality and public equality, are sources of contradictions in relation to Muslims. More precisely, the multicultural interpretation of equality between religions, paralleling arguments of equality between the genders and between racial, ethnic and cultural groups, seems to lead in the direction of active policies of inclusion of Muslims (and others) rather than a principled indifference to organised religion. Hence, the claims of religious equality are not decisively in alignment with some readings of secularist principles. We must therefore explore some meanings of multiculturalism and their implications for the public/private distinction.[12]

Multiculturalism and the strict division between public and private spheres

There is a body of theoretical opinion that argues that the public/private distinction is essential to multiculturalism. John Rex, for example, distinguishes between plural societies such as apartheid South Africa and the multicultural ideal. He contends that the fundamental distinction between them is that the latter restricts cultural diversity to a private sphere so all enjoy equality of opportunity and uniform treatment in the public domain.[13] Immigrants and minorities do not have to respect the normative power of a dominant culture, but there must be a normative universality in relation to law, politics, economics and welfare policy.

An important assumption contained in this way of seeing the public/private distinction is found in a discussion by Habermas. Although he maintains that a recipient society cannot require immigrants to assimilate (immigrants cannot be obliged to conform to the dominant way of life) he also contends that a democratic constitutional regime must seek to

> preserve the identity of the political community, which nothing, including immigration, can be permitted to encroach upon, since that identity is founded on the constitutional principles anchored in the political culture and not on the basic ethical orientations of the cultural form of life predominant in that country.[14]

But is this distinction between the political and cultural identities of a society valid? Politics and law depend to some degree on shared ethical assumptions and inevitably reflect the norms and values of the society they are part of. In this sense, no regime stands outside culture, ethnicity or nationality, and changes in these will need to be reflected in the political arrangements of the regime. Indeed, Habermas seems to concede this when he states that 'as other forms of life become established [i.e. following immigration] the horizon within which citizens henceforth interpret their common constitutional principles may also expand'.[15] But this concession begs the question of the coherence of his initial distinction. If the political identity of the regime is determined by reference to the 'constitutional principles anchored in the political culture', how can the articulation, interpretation and, therefore, operation of these constitutional principles not be subject to the 'basic ethical orientations' of new (religious) citizens, given these orientations provide the fundamental interpretative horizons for these principles? As the fundamental interpretative horizons of the citizenry 'expand' through the immigration of peoples with religions new to that society, so too the political identity of the regime is inevitably altered. Moreover, the interdependence between the political and the cultural, the public and the private, is not confined to the level of ethical generalities. On a practical level, as Rex recognises, religious communities may look to the state to support their culture (for example, through support for religious schools and other educational institutions) and the state may, reciprocally, look to religious communities to inculcate virtues such as truthtelling, respect for property, service to others, and so on, without which a civic morality would have nothing to build on.

Furthermore, if the public and private spheres mutually shape each other in these ways, then however 'abstract' and 'rational' the principles of a public order may be, they will reflect the 'folk cultures' out of which that particular public order has grown. If this is the case, then, there can be no question of the public sphere being morally, ethnically or, indeed, religiously neutral. Rather, it will inevitably appeal to points of privately shared values and a sense of belonging found within the (religious and non-religious) communities that make up society, as well as to the superstructure of conventions, laws and principles which regulate it. And this can be so not only in the absence of any official state recognition of (a) religion but even in the absence of widespread adherence to historical state religions. Norris and Inglehart make this point well and are worth quoting at length:

> The distinctive worldviews that were originally linked with religious traditions have shaped the cultures of each nation in an enduring fashion; today these distinctive values are transmitted to the citizens even if they never set foot in a church, temple, or mosque. Thus, although only about 5% of the Swedish public attends church weekly, the Swedish public as a whole manifests a distinctive Protestant value system that they hold in common with the citizens of other historically Protestant societies such as Norway, Denmark, Iceland, Finland, Germany, and the Netherlands. Today, these values are not transmitted primarily by the church, but by the educational system and the mass media, with the result that although the value systems of historically Protestant countries differ markedly and consistently from those of historically Catholic countries – the value system of Dutch Catholics are much more similar to those of Dutch Protestants than to those of French, Italian, or Spanish Catholics. Even in highly secular societies, the historical legacy of given religions continues to shape worldviews and to define cultural zones. As a distinguished Estonian colleague put it, in explaining the difference between the worldviews of Estonians and Russians, 'We are all atheists; but I am a Lutheran atheist, and they are Orthodox atheists.'[16]

This will have the important implication that those citizens whose moral, ethnic or religious communal identities are most adequately reflected in the political identity of the regime, those citizens whose private identity fits most comfortably with this political identity, will feel least the force of a rigidly enforced public/private distinction. They may only become aware of its coercive influence when they have to share the public domain with persons from other communities, persons who may also wish the identity of the political community to reflect something of their own community too.

There is, therefore, a real possibility that the elaboration of a strict public/private distinction may simply act to buttress the privileged position of the historically 'integrated' folk cultures at the expense of the historically subordinated or newly migrated folk. This will not be equality between religions. In some contexts, therefore, a strict interpretation and application of the public/private distinction, far from underpinning multiculturalism, will work to prevent its emergence.

Public/private interdependence and the politics of recognition

If we recognise that the public sphere is not morally neutral, that the public order is not culturally, religiously or ethnically blind, we can begin to understand why oppressed, marginalised or immigrant groups may want that public order (in which they may for the first time have rights of participation) to 'recognise' them, to be 'user-friendly' to the new folks. The logic of demanding that public institutions acknowledge their ways of doing things becomes readily intelligible, as does the whole phenomenon of minorities seeking increased visibility, of contesting the boundaries of the public, of not simply asking to be left alone and to be civilly tolerated.

What is important to recognise here is that the content of what is claimed today in the name of equality is more than that which would have been claimed in the 1960s. Iris Young expresses the new political climate when she describes the emergence of an ideal of equality based not just on allowing excluded groups to assimilate and live by the norms of dominant groups, but also on the view that 'a positive self-definition of group difference is in fact more liberatory'.[17] She cites the examples of the black power movement, the gay pride assertion that sexual identity is a matter of culture and politics, and a feminism that emphasises the positivity and specificity of female experience and values. Although these movements have not had the same impact in Europe as in parts of North America, they are nevertheless present here.

The shift in the content of these claims is from an understanding of equality in terms of individualism and cultural assimilation to a politics of recognition, to equality as encompassing public ethnicity. That is to say, equality as not having to hide or apologise for one's origins, family or community, but requiring others to show respect for them and adapt public attitudes and arrangements so that the heritage they represent is encouraged rather than ignored or expected to wither away.

There seem, then, to be two distinct conceptions of equal citizenship, with each based on a different view of what is 'public' and 'private'. Broadly speaking, the first equates with the content of the claims for equality proffered in the 1960s, the second accords more fully with the content of the claims presented by contemporary proponents of a politics of recognition. These two conceptions of equality may be stated as follows:

1. The right to assimilate to the majority/dominant culture in the public sphere; and toleration of 'difference' in the private sphere.
2. The right to have one's 'difference' (minority ethnicity, etc.) recognised and supported in the public and the private spheres.

These two conceptions are not mutually exclusive. Indeed, multiculturalism requires support for both conceptions. For the assumption behind the first conception is that participation in the public or national culture is necessary for the effective exercise of citizenship (the only obstacles to which are the exclusionary processes preventing gradual assimilation). The second conception, too, assumes groups excluded from the public or national culture have their citizenship diminished as a result but proposes to remedy this by offering the right to assimilate while, at the same time, agreeing to widen and adapt the public or national culture (including the public and media symbols of national membership) to incorporate the relevant minority ethnicities.

It may be thought the second conception of equality involves something of a contradiction: it accepts that participation in national or shared culture(s) is necessary for effective equality but encourages individuals to cultivate minority identities and practices. There is indeed a genuine tension here, and perhaps it can only be resolved in practice, through finding and cultivating points of common ground between dominant and subordinate cultures, as well as new syntheses and hybridities. For an effective multicultural interaction, the important thing is this tension should not be heightened by the burdens of change (or the costs of not changing) all falling on one party to the encounter.

This leaves open as to who is to count as a relevant minority, who is allowed to make claims and is granted recognition? While different factors are relevant, 'difference' is not straightforwardly given but arises out of the interaction between a group and the sociopolitical context, which creates salience and establishes the limits of visibility or legitimacy. This explains why in some countries religion has come to the fore and in particular that Islam has become a core element for minority community construction and a source of group mobilisation.[18] The claim for equality and justice for Muslims thus often stems from the exclusion of religious associations from the process of resource distribution, while at the same time allowing religion to exist in and mobilise in civil society. At other times, it is the political marginalisation or demotion of religious identity in favour of allegedly more acceptable identities, such as those of race and gender, that creates the grievances of misrecognition. The issue is not the cultural assimilation of individual immigrants but the recognition of group identities, in this case, a religious community. Certainly, the idea of equality as respect for difference has created a sociopolitical climate in which non-assimilation at a sociocultural level is in many countries not regarded as a problem, and even in France the ideology and the term 'assimilation' with regard to culture has been replaced by integration. Moreover, institutionalisation of a difference, whatever this difference might be, has emerged as a legitimate way of responding to new cultural and religious communities. The question of recognition of differences is therefore the same as how to assimilate/integrate difference institutionally. This leaves open the possibility that the state responds to the new presence of Islam through a form of structural assimilation or, paralleling integration at the level of civil society, in a more flexible way. The authors are divided on what form this structural assimilation may take. For Modood, institutional integration can take a pluralistic form, a variable geometry, in which Islam is integrated in ways that reflect existing national arrangements as well as the character of local Muslim needs and capacities. This reflects the experience of England, in which the Church of England, the Catholic Church, Protestant churches such as the Methodists, as well as Judaism, all enjoy some kind of state recognition and resources in relation to Parliament, schooling, the armed forces, hospitals, prisons and so on, but the relationship in each case is a product of its own history and population distribution. Thus, for Modood, if British Islam remains as decentralised and unhierarchical as it has started, then this should be taken into account in the political and structural accommodation that is offered to it in Britain. For Kastoryano, on the other hand, whatever the degree of cultural pluralism that becomes the norm in civil society, the state must promote equality and symmetry at the level of national representative institutions. As the existing arrangements in France require each nationally recognised faith community to have a representative structure with 'chiefs' representing a national membership, so French Islam must conform to this pattern. It may be that this runs counter to Sunni Islam, with its traditions of autonomous mosques and sects, but it is the duty of French Muslim organisations to assimilate by producing representative structures that allow the state to extend recognition to Islam without compromising its symmetrical and equitable structures.[19] This would mean that Islam would be assimilated on an equal footing to all representative religious institutions in France. The result would be a genuinely French Islam and its freedom from foreign influences, especially the politics of countries of origin.

Pluralistic institutional integration/assimilation

Multicultural equality, then, when applied to religious groups means that secularism *simpliciter* can be an obstacle to pluralistic integration and equality. This does not, however, mean that there is an irreconcilable conflict between secularism and multicultural equality because, as we have seen, secularism pure and simple is not what exists in the world. The country-by-country situation is more complex, and indeed, far less inhospitable to the accommodation of Muslims than the ideology of secularism (or, for that matter, the ideology of anti-secularism) might suggest.[20] All actual practices of secularism consist of institutional compromises and these can, should be and are being extended to accommodate Muslims. The institutional reconfiguration varies according to the place of religion therefore of Islam in each country developed earlier. Today the appropriate response to the new Muslim challenges is pluralistic institutional integration/assimilation, rather than an appeal to a radical public–private separation in the name of secularism. The approach that is being argued for here, then, consists of:

1. A reconceptualisation of secularism from the concepts of neutrality and the strict public/private divide to a moderate and evolutionary secularism based on institutional adjustments;

2. A reconceptualisation of equality from sameness to an incorporation of a respect for difference;
3. A pragmatic, case by case, negotiated approach to dealing with controversy and conflict, not an ideological, drawing a 'line in the sand' mentality.

This institutional integration/assimilation approach is based on including Islam in the institutional framework of the state, using the historical accommodation between state and Church as a basis for negotiations in order to achieve consensual resolutions consistent with equality and justice. As these accommodations have varied from country to country, it means there is no exemplary solution, for contemporary solutions too will depend on the national context and will not have a once-and-for-all-time basis. It is clearly a dialogical perspective and assumes the possibility of mutual education and learning. Like all negotiation and reform, there are normative as well as practical limits. Aspects of the former have been usefully characterised by Bhikhu Parekh as 'society's operative public values'.[21] These values, such as equality between the sexes, are embedded in the political constitution, in specific laws and in the norms governing the civic relations in a society. Norms, laws and constitutional principles concerning the appropriate place of religion in public life generally and in specific policy areas (such as schools or rehabilitation of criminals) consist of such public values and are reasoned about, justified or criticised by reference to specific values about religion/politics as well as more general norms and values in a society, such as fairness, or balance or consensus and so on. We, therefore, recognise that the approach recommended here involves solutions that are highly contextual and practical but they are far from arbitrary or without reference to values. While the latter are not static because they are constantly being reinterpreted, realigned, extended and reformed, nevertheless they provide a basis for dialogue and agreement.

The institutional integration/assimilation that we are advocating is possible and is taking place to some extent, despite the presence sometimes of a vigorous version of secularism in the national political culture, especially among intellectuals.[22] For example, while in France there has been a revival of the old duality between religion and state in public discussions and some policies, at the same time the climate of controversy has accelerated the establishment of a representative institution of Islam on an equal footing with other religions. Since the first headscarf affair in the late 1980s, the concept of *laïcité* has gone through different interpretations with Islam serving as a mirror to its ambiguity and contradictions, and highlighting that in the French polity religion is the main and long-term 'difference' that enjoys institutional recognition. For the separation of Church and state confers institutional legal status on the Catholic clergy, the Protestants of the National Federation of the Protestant Churches of France, and to the Jews governed by the Consistory. That 'recognition' is seen as an expression of respect for freedom of religion and the neutrality of the secular state. Since 1990, following the passionate debates concerning the place of religion in French society aroused by the headscarf affair, successive interior ministers, who are at the same time ministers of religion from both the Left and the Right, have worked to create representative Islamic institutions. In 1991, Pierre Joxe created a Council of Thought on Islam in France, the CORIF, in order to explore different means of adapting the requirements of Islam to the norms of society (or vice versa). The next minister, Charles Pasqua, of the Rally for the Republic (RPR), created a Representative Council of Muslims, with the idea that 'the issue of Islam must be treated as a French issue'. He declared in *Le Monde* of 11 January 1995: 'I have always wanted Islam to progress from the status of a tolerated religion in France to that of a religion accepted by all, and one that forms part of the French spiritual landscape.' His successor, Jean-Pierre Chevènement (Socialist Party) also declared that the recognition of Islam was 'not a question of left or right but a national question which affects the Republican state' and set up a commission called a 'Consultation' that also gave its name to a journal. In the first issue of that journal he declared his goal was to 'help Muslims to form themselves into a religious minority in France'. Most recently, in April 2003, Interior Minister Nicolas Sarkozy succeeded in creating a French Council of the Muslim Faith (Conseil Français du Culte Musulman), which subsequently elected its first national representative.

The institutional approach is obviously an important way to achieve equality and representation for religious groups. Bringing Muslims into historic and existing institutional arrangements means a continuity with the old French scheme described by Danièle Lochak of a 'pragmatic handling of differences'. This consists of gradually introducing the minimal dose of institutionalisation needed for a concrete resolution of the practical problems created by the existence of 'minority groups' who want to end up with 'official recognition', which would then produce the institutionalisation of differences.[23] What is interesting about France is that while republican ideology is meant to be blind to 'difference', above all to religious difference, in its institutional architecture France not only recognises difference at the level of organised religion but recognises no other form of group difference to anything like the same degree. As Lochak states, 'the state's ignoring of the prohibition of differences is confined to religion', and that while France rejects the notion of 'minority' in all other contexts, the term 'religious minority' appears in legal texts.[24] This suggests to us that religion is (*pace* republican ideology) one of the fundamental cleavages in French society and its social, cultural and institutional representation.[25] The current effort to recognise Islam institutionally, then, is based in principle on the idea of equality of treatment of all religions in France, including the Catholic clergy.

Having seen that this is happening in a state that made *laicité* its particularity, France, it is only to be expected that this is happening in other European states too. This includes the development of a religious equality agenda in Britain, including the incorporation of some Muslim schools on the same basis as schools of religions with a much longer presence. It also includes the recommendations of the Royal Commission on the Reform of the House of Lords (2000) that in addition to the Anglican bishops who sit in that House by right as part of the Anglican 'establishment', this right should be extended to cover those of other Christian and non-Christian faiths. The same point can be made in relation to the fact that as early as 1974 the Belgian state decided to include Islam within its Council of Religions as a full member, or to the way that Muslims in the Netherlands have long had state-funded religious schools and television channels as a progressive step in that country's traditional way of institutionally dealing with organised religion, namely, 'pillarisation'. This principle that recognised that Protestants and Catholics had a right to state resources and some publicly funded autonomous institutions officially ended in 1960. It is, however, still considered as a 'relevant framework for the development of a model that grants certain collective rights to religious groups'[26] in such matters as state funding of Islamic schools. So, the accommodation of Muslims is being achieved through a combination of pillarisation and Dutch minority policies. In Germany, the question of the public recognition of Islam was raised as early as the 1980s, based on a definition of 'community' offered by the *Ausländerbeauftragte*, the Commission on Foreigners, as 'a grouping of people who feel that they are linked to one or several deities and which eventually give rise to a faith'. This religious conception of community dates back to the nineteenth century when the religious freedom granted to both Catholics and Lutherans took on the corporate character of 'granting equal rights to communities constituted into organized bodies'.[27] Recognition by public authorities of a 'Muslim community' was, therefore, suggested as a means of integrating Turkish immigrants into German society. The argument was firmly based on the official place of religion in German public space and the role of churches in taking care of foreigners in the manner of a 'religious society' (*Religionsgesellschaft*). It was appealed to by the Confederation of Islamic Cultural Centres in 1979 when it presented a request for recognition within the corporate body of public law (*Körperschaft des öffentlichen Rechts*) by the Islamic Federation of Berlin, hoping for recognition as *Religionsgemeinschaft* in the *Land* of Berlin in 1980, a status it finally won in 2000.[28] This precedent is being appealed to in other *Länder*.[29] Of course that is not to say that steps such as these were without controversy or that there is a simple, linear development.

We have not attempted to discuss here in a comprehensive way the kinds of legal and policy measures that are necessary to accommodate Muslims as equal citizens in France, Britain and other European polities. These would include anti-discrimination measures in areas such as employment, positive action to achieve a full and just political representation of Muslims in various areas of public life, the inclusion of Muslim history as European history and so on. We have just been considering the inclusion of Islam as an organised religion and of Muslim identity as a public identity. Our argument has been that such inclusion is necessary to integrate Muslims and to pursue religious equality. While this inclusion runs against certain interpretations of secularism, it is not inconsistent with what secularism means in practice in Europe. We should let the letter and the spirit of compromise that it represents be our guide and not an ideological secularism that is unfortunately generating European domestic versions of 'the clash of civilisations' thesis and the conflicts that entails for European societies. The fact that some people are today developing secularism as an ideology to oppose Islam and its public recognition, is a challenge both to pluralism and equality, and thus to some of the bases of contemporary democracy.

Notes

1. A version of this chapter was first published in T. Modood, A. Triandafyllidou and R. Zapata-Barrero (eds), *Multiculturalism, Muslims and Citizenship: a European Approach* (London: Routledge, 2006).
2. A special clause in the treaty allowed the two religions of the Empire, Catholicism and Protestantism, to live together.

3. H. Müller, 'De l'Aufklärung à Weimar. Mouvement des idées et mutations politiques', in A.-M. LeGloannec (ed.), *L'État de l'Allemagne* (Paris: La Découverte, 1995), pp. 33–7.
4. E. François, *Protestants et catholiques en Allemagne. Identités et pluralisme, Augsbourg 1648–1806* (Paris: Albin Michel, 1993), p. 239.
5. N.D de Graaf and A. Need, 'Losing Faith: Is Britain Alone', in R. Jowell et al. (eds), *British Social Attitudes: Focusing on Diversity*, The 17th Report (London: Sage, 2000).
6. P. Schuck, *Diversity in America: Keeping Government at a Safe Distance* (Cambridge, Mass.: Harvard University Press, 2003).
7. M. Sandel, 'Review of Rawls' *Political Liberalism*', *Harvard Law Review*, 107 (1994), pp. 1765–94; see also P. Hamburger, *Separation of Church and State* (Cambridge, Mass.: Harvard University Press, 2002).
8. A. Greely, 'The Persistence of Religion', *Cross Currents*, 45 (1995), pp. 24–41.
9. C. Nicolet, *L'Idée républicaine en France (1789–1924)* (Paris: Gallimard, 1995).
10. Ibid.
11. T. Modood, 'Establishment, Multiculturalism and British Citizenship', *Political Quarterly*, 65/1 (1994), pp. 53–73; see also T. Modood, *Church, State and Religious Minorities* (London: Policy Studies, 1997).
12. T. Modood, 'Multiculturalism, Secularism and the State', *Critical Review of International, Social and Political Philosophy*, 1/3 (1998), pp. 79–97; in R. Bellamy and M. Hollis (eds), *Pluralism and Liberal Neutrality* (London: Frank Cass, 1999).
13. J. Rex, *Race and Ethnicity* (Milton Keynes: Open University Press, 1986), Ch. 7.
14. J. Habermas, 'Struggles for Recognition in the Democratic Constitutional State', in A. Gutmann (ed.), *Multiculturalism: Examining the Politics of Recognition* (Princeton: Princeton University Press, 1994), p. 139.
15. Ibid., pp. 139–40.
16. P. Norris and R. Inglehart, *Sacred and Secular: Religion and Politics Worldwide* (Cambridge: Cambridge University Press, 2004). Separate from this but also relevant is how the presence of assertive Muslim identities may be stimulating a revival of Christian cultural identities without a revival of Christian religious practices (e.g. see D. Voas and S. Bruce, 'The 2001 Census and Christian Identification in Britain', *Journal of Contemporary Religion*, 19/1 (2004), pp. 23–8).
17. I.M. Young, *Justice and the Politics of Difference* (Princeton: Princeton University Press, 1990), p. 157.
18. R. Kastoryano, *Negotiating Identities: States and Immigrants in France and Germany* (Princeton: Princeton University Press, 2002).
19. R. Kastoryano, 'Religion and Incorporation. Islam in France and Germany', *International Migration Review*, Fall (2004), pp. 1234–56.
20. T. Modood, 'Multiculturalism, Secularism and the State', Table 1; reproduced in Bellamy and Hollis, *Pluralism and Liberal Neutrality*.
21. B. Parekh, *Rethinking Multiculturalism: Cultural Diversity and Political Theory* (Basingstoke: Palgrave Macmillan, 2000), p. 267.
22. We are not suggesting that it is merely a question of state ideology and state action. Sometimes difficulties arise from Muslim organisations, especially the competition between them, and sometimes from the intervention of

the country of origin, such as Turkey in relation to Germany or Morocco in relation to France.
23. D. Lochak, 'Les minorités dans le droit public français: du refus des différences à la gestion des différences', *Conditions des minorités depuis 1789*, CRISPA-GDM (Paris: L'Harmattan, 1989).
24. Ibid., pp. 111–84. Even that very 'republican' Minister of Interior of the late 1990s, Jean-Pierre Chevènement, declared that he would like to see Islam 'develop in France as a minority religion like the Jews and Protestants', *Consultation*, no. 1 (2000).
25. This is potentially a dynamic process: Muslims appeal to the institutional recognition given over many decades and longer to Christians and Jews, while the latter may at times be stimulated to strengthen a weakening institutional position by supporting Muslim demands or even by asking for extra powers in the context of the revisiting of state-religion arrangements prompted by the claims-making of Muslims.
26. T. Sunier and M. von Luijeren, 'Islam in the Netherlands', in Y. Haddad (ed.), *Muslims in the West. From Sojourners to Citizens* (New York: Oxford University Press, 2002), pp. 144–58.
27. E. François, *Protestants et catholiques en Allemagne. Identités et pluralisme, Augsbourg 1648–1806* (Paris: Albin Michel, 1993).
28. See *Deutsches Verwaltungsblatt* 1.7.2000: Die Bremer Klausel des Art. 141 GG gilt in ganz Berlin, S. 1001–6. Recognition, however, has raised questions about the place of Islam in state education, just as with the Christian faiths. Since the 1990s, attempts have been made in three *Länder* to integrate Islam into the public schools. In Berlin, since religious instruction, by and large, is associated with the churches, instruction of the Koran has been placed under the supervision of the Turkish state through the intermediary of the Diyanet, its official organ. The presence of Islamic instructors has since 1984 been included in the bilateral agreements that initially governed the provision of Turkish language classes. In Hamburg, a Social Democratic (SPD) *Land*, language teachers, even of Turkish nationality, enjoy the status of civil servants, and have established instruction in Islam within the *Religionspedagogik* programme that applies to all religions. In northern Westphalia, teachers of theology, scientists and Christian pedagogues are responsible for implementing a curriculum of Islam.
29. C. De Galembert and N. Tietze, 'Institutionalisierung desIslam in Deutschland. Pluralisierung der Weltanschauungen', *Mittelweg*, 36, 11/1 (2002), pp. 43–62.

Select bibliography

Bellamy, R. and Hollis, M. (eds), *Pluralism and Liberal Neutrality* (London: Frank Cass and Co., 1999).
De Galembert, C. and Tietze, N., 'Institutionalisierung desIslam in Deutschland. Pluralisierung der Weltanschauungen', *Mittelweg*, 36, 11/1 (2002), pp. 43–62.
De Graaf, N.D. and Need, A., 'Losing Faith: Is Britain Alone', in Jowell, R. et al. (eds), *British Social Attitudes: Focusing on Diversity*, The 17th Report (London: Sage, 2000).

32   *The Construction of Minority Identities in France and Britain*

François, E., *Protestants et catholiques en Allemagne. Identités et pluralisme, Augsbourg 1648–1806* (Paris: Albin Michel, 1993).

Greely, A., 'The Persistence of Religion', *Cross Currents*, 45 (1995), pp. 24–41.

Habermas, J., 'Struggles for Recognition in the Democratic Constitutional State' in Gutmann, A. (ed), *Multiculturalism: Examining the Politics of Recognition* (Princeton: Princeton University Press, 1994).

Haddad, Y. (ed.), *Muslims in the West. From Sojourners to Citizens* (New York: Oxford University Press, 2002).

Hamburger, P., *Separation of Church and State* (Cambridge, Mass.: Harvard University Press, 2002).

Kastoryano, R., 'Religion and Incorporation. Islam in France and Germany', *International Migration Review*, Fall (2004), pp. 1234–56.

—— *Negotiating Identities: States and Immigrants in France and Germany* (Princeton: Princeton University Press, 2002).

LeGloannec, A.-M., (ed.), *L'État de l'Allemagne* (Paris: La Découverte, 1995).

Lochak, D., 'Les minorités dans le droit public français: du refus des différences à la gestion des différences', in *Conditions des minorités depuis 1789*, CRISPA-GDM (Paris: L'Harmattan, 1989).

Modood, T. (ed.), *Church, State and Religious Minorities* (London: Policy Studies, 1997).

Nicolet, C., *L'Idée républicaine en France (1789–1924)* (Paris: Gallimard, 1995).

Norris, P. and Inglehart, R., *Sacred and Secular: Religion and Politics Worldwide* (Cambridge: Cambridge University Press, 2004).

Parekh, B., *Rethinking Multiculturalism: Cultural Diversity and Political Theory* (Basingstoke: Palgrave Macmillan, 2000).

Rex, J., *Race and Ethnicity* (Milton Keynes: Open University Press, 1986).

Royal Commission on the Reform of the House of Lords, *A House for the Future* (London: HMSO, 2000).

Sandel, M., 'Review of Rawls' *Political Liberalism*', *Harvard Law Review*, 107 (1994), pp. 1765–94.

Voas, D. and Bruce, S., 'The 2001 Census and Christian Identification in Britain', *Journal of Contemporary Religion*, 19/1 (2004), pp. 23–8.

Young, I. M., *Justice and the Politics of Difference* (Princeton: Princeton University Press, 1990).

2
The Construction of What?
Michel Wieviorka

Introduction

In the space of 40 years, since the mid-1960s, one question which has come to the fore in many societies (and it is a genuinely 'global' question since it involves issues which are at once general, worldwide and local), is that of cultural differences, for example ethnic or religious differences. In some cases, as we see in particular with Islam, these are in a position to challenge world order, and the functioning of many countries, possibly even of many regional or local political systems.

In the first instance, these differences were mainly seen as questions of reproduction. We wondered whether the demands for the recognition of cultural identities in the public sphere were not perhaps natural, or at least purely inherited, fundamental and rooted in a distant past, in time immemorial; they were sometimes considered to be 'primary' or 'primordial'. This point of view, which links the naturalisation of culture with an approach conceived in terms of reproduction, was widespread, even if in the field of anthropology or history it met with resistance and a tendency to speak instead of the 'invention of traditions'. The consequence of defining various human groups in terms of their cultural essence or nature meant that this was seen uniquely as a heritage from the past which might, or might not, be able to withstand economic or political forces which could only beset and weaken them, like money, for example, which undermines cultures, or Jacobinism, which imposes the rule of central government on political constituencies and peripheral groups. In many societies, including the two which are the focus of this study, France and the United Kingdom, immigration reinforced this vision. It seemed to bring with it cultural specificities from afar, both in terms of space and of time; some doubted whether immigrants were capable of integrating into the host society and its nation. Cultural or differentialist racism, sometimes referred to as 'new racism', is one of the common ways of perceiving these cultural identities which the various waves of immigration apparently brought with them; the postulate is that the targeted groups are culturally apart, the bearers of differences which are irreducible because they are rooted almost naturally in their personalities.

This vision was also sometimes part of the widespread theme of 'revival', an idea which applies to all sorts of phenomena, including ethnicity and religion. Anthony Smith, for example, insisted on 'the ethnical revival in the modern world',[1] while others spoke of the return of the 'revenge of God'.[2] To evoke a 'revival' means, in effect, to evoke the possibility of seeing a phenomenon returning from the past with renewed vigour and vitality when it seemed to have disappeared. Finally, from this perspective, modernity is seen as being opposed to tradition and, in the last resort, can be reduced to the image of a conflict between the universal values of the rule of law and of reason and the specific values of groups characterised by their archaism and pre-modern forms of solidarity and existence. This conception, inherited from the Enlightenment and the nineteenth century, is based on the idea of an evolution in which the forces of modernity advance whereas traditions and archaism only decline; it is inherent in the idea of progress and in philosophies of history which insist on the inevitable decline of the forces of tradition. This conception is an inherent part of evolutionism. Furthermore, this conception of modernity has itself, paradoxically, been reinforced by a relativist variant, in which the same image of a conflict between specificities and the universal values of modernity is maintained, but the political or philosophical judgement is reversed; here tradition is defended against the inroads of progress and instrumental reason. We learn, for example, that 'small is beautiful', and in extreme forms of relativism, specific cultures are valorised by challenging universal values.

Whatever the case may be, the idea that cultural differences can be reduced to a process of reproduction has been constantly challenged, particularly in the social sciences, to the point that it now appears to be so totally unsuited to the phenomenon which it claims to describe that it has been almost abandoned.

The rise of differences

The social sciences have indeed taken up the issues posed by the collective demands emanating from various identities and suggested analyses which are very far from the ideological set of representations in the evolutionist approach or those which stress the reproduction of cultural specificities. Throughout the 1980s and 1990s, they opposed this notion of reproduction by suggesting instead various types of invention or construction, stressing the fact that not only are cultural identities invented and even possibly, in Lévi-Strauss's terms, 'cobbled together',[3] but also that disintegrated forms which, for example, include racist or fundamentalist elements, are also forms of production. Thus, for example in the Anglo-Saxon world, more than in France where people hesitate to use the word 'race', there is frequent recourse to the idea that races are man-made constructions and are not natural; they are in these instances frequently defined as social products, and not in terms of some inherent essence, thus making the actual word 'race' more acceptable.

Considerable intellectual progress has thus enabled us to advance in the understanding of cultural differences and has moreover contributed to advancing political and institutional thinking. It is important therefore to signal the key elements in the changes that have occurred.

The first point concerns the relationship, at first sight paradoxical, between the rise in collective identities and that of modern individualism. One could spontaneously conceive of these two phenomena as being opposed, with the former referring to the image of societies organised on the basis of groups constituted in the form of communities or minorities which are visible and active in the public sphere and the latter offering, on the contrary, the image of widespread individualism, leaving little room for community action and even destroying it. But this conception is erroneous for a very simple reason: modern individualism nurtures community identities, it does not destroy them. In the past, when identities were reproduced, individuals had little choice: the group, in the name of tradition, subjected them to its law and each individual was little more than an atom of a social entity perpetuating itself as such. But nowadays, there is an increasing desire on the part of individuals to choose their identity, including that of community; they participate as individuals (and therefore may also want to leave) sharing the values of the group to which they consider they belong as a result of their personal decision. To give a simple example: in the past, a young Muslim was a Muslim because his or her parents, grandparents, etc. were Muslims; nowadays, he or she will explain to the researcher interviewing him or her that his or her religion is their own choice, the outcome of a decision made individually. Another way of saying this is that an understanding of the major contemporary forms of identity must include individualism in its dimensions of personal subjectivity and, consequently, the work of the individual subject. This puts an end to the evolutionist arguments referred to above: modernity today (even if we want to call it 'post-modernity' and I do not intend here to go into these discussions which ended in the 1980s and 1990s) is not the triumph of individualism, of reason and of the rule of law, over collective identities and all that they involve in the way of passions and reinvented traditions, nor the contrary, the return to traditions or to tribal organisation. Rather, it tends to be a question of the tension between these two registers, between the demands of the individual, of reason and the rule of law and that of groups, passions, convictions and traditions.

The second point to consider is the separation between the cultural and the social. The question might have remained theoretical if the implementation of multiculturalist policies had not provided an answer, or rather, two answers. What does this signify? It is a question of knowing how far the analysis has to distinguish between declarations or demands of a cultural nature (by which I mean, for example, that my identity be recognised in the public sphere), and the concerns or expectations of a social nature (for example, I challenge the social inequality to which I am subjected). To amalgamate these two registers is to confuse dimensions which everyone, from personal experience, knows very well to be distinct, but to separate them completely implies that there is no direct link between them. However, research demonstrates that they are constantly linked. For example, in France, the rise of the Front National, which stresses the cultural identity of the French nation, cannot be explained without seeing that it is expressed by people who are downwardly socially mobile, or who fear they may become so, or who wish to differentiate themselves from those who are poor. Another example is the rise of Islam in France, which cannot be understood unless there is an understanding of the social conditions, the exclusion and the racism to which the populations of North African immigrant origin are subjected. This does not mean that religious belief and convictions can be explained by social factors, which is another problem. In some cases, demands for recognition and for cultural rights have nothing to do with social demands. For example, when the Armenian communities demand that the French government recognise the 1915 Armenian genocide, they never in any way refer to social difficulties or injustice. But it is frequently the same people who are subject to a lack of cultural recognition and to social inequalities and who are at one and the same time denied their cultural existence and treated as second-class citizens or excluded socially.

If we decide to deal with these two problems, should we implement a single policy or two separate policies? In the 1970s some countries, beginning with Canada and Australia, opted for what could be called an 'integrated' multiculturalism which consisted in simultaneously granting cultural rights to minorities and in helping their members in various areas in social life such as employment, housing, and access to health services, etc. On the other hand, in the United States we can speak of a 'fragmented' multiculturalism: demands for cultural recognition are one thing, social demands are another. Thus what are known as 'affirmative action' measures have nothing to do with cultural recognition. For example, black Americans are not told that they are being recognised as 'African-Americans' for their music, their literature, their history, etc., but these policies offer them special means of access, to universities, for example. They are social policies for the benefit of individuals who belong to minorities who may well mobilise to obtain cultural rights at another point in time, but not necessarily.

Finally, the third important thing that we have learnt over time is linked to the fact that we have a better understanding of how to distinguish between the registers and not to confuse the three different levels. Analysing the emergence of cultural differences, the conditions for their rise, the internal tensions to which they are subject, the demands and the challenges which they formulate, the conflicts which they arouse, whether, for example, the forms they assume are open or closed for example (communitarianism, fundamentalism, racism and so on) is one thing. Expressing value judgements is altogether different, discussing what is just or unjust for them, good or bad, and therefore saying which policies would be desirable or otherwise for them. And any suggestions of appropriate policies based on a definition of what is good or bad, just or unjust, good and evil are yet again something else. In the first case, the social sciences and primarily sociology have to be mobilised; the second situation is the domain of political philosophy; the third sphere is that of political science. These three types of approach should not be confused: setting out an analysis is one thing, suggesting guidelines for action is another and implementing a policy, for example, multiculturalism, is a third.

Changes

Throughout the 1970s, 1980s and 1990s there were heated discussions, first in the field of political philosophy and then in the sphere of politics, properly speaking, and later in the social sciences specifically. This led to extensive discussions in which the 'liberals' confronted the 'communitarians' in the Anglo-Saxon world and in France, to use Régis Debray's terminology, which dates from the mid-1980s, the 'democrats' confronted the 'republicans'.[4] These discussions did not come to any conclusion but they are now over; no new arguments have really been put forward for several years. Similarly, multiculturalism was discussed and even opposed in the areas in which it was implemented but there again, while this type of policy does continue to be a controversial subject and one which is discussed, there has been little advance in the formulation of arguments. We observe that in the countries with 'integrated' multiculturalism the accompanying passions gradually petered out as its importance as a policy declined but did not necessarily disappear: in the United States it has been weakened but on the other hand, in a country like France, we could say there has been a timid and modest advance in 'fragmented' multiculturalism with steps recently which should not be exaggerated both in the field of policies for cultural recognition and for 'positive discrimination', i.e. the French version of the American expression 'affirmative action'. But nevertheless, important changes must be taken into consideration.

A framework for analysis

The first set of changes relates to the framework within which cultural differences are considered. Classically, considerations and discussions here function within the bounds of states and nations. Thus, I have just referred to France, Canada, the United States, the United Kingdom, etc. But this is not necessarily the most appropriate context. Nowadays, cultural differences are rapidly transnational and are established, in various modes, in numerous countries. Old diasporas continue and others are created, such as that of the 'black Atlantic' which Paul Gilroy described back in the 1990s.[5] Complex transfrontier networks are at play, associating forms of cultural life and economic practices, sometimes delineating what Alain Tarrius has referred to as globalisation 'from below', with countless people of North African immigrant origin circulating like ants, in this instance, all round the Mediterranean basin, and far beyond, and developing forms of trade while simultaneously avoiding ghettoisation which, otherwise, is a frequent threat. The model for both the analysis and the discussion from the 1970s to the 1990s is constructed on differences that may exist within the confines of the nation state (for example in France: Bretons, Corsicans...), or may have entered and settled, usually willingly (immigrants) but sometimes forming an 'unwilling' minority to use the expression John Ogbu coined to describe the black Americans of slave origin;[6] yet others, for example, in the case of homosexuals, have been invented. But this model is incomplete; it does not include the diasporas, the movements backwards and forwards, the phenomena of transit, the formation of frontier regions, etc. How should we consider, for example the experience of the descendants of the Japanese immigrants in Brazil, who 'return' to Japan but do not intend to remain there, and then go to Canada or Australia? They live in Japan with a feeling of experiencing racism despite their physical appearance, which is Japanese, and they remain very attached to Brazil. Can we reduce the presence of Mexicans in the United States to a simple problem of 'Mexican-Americans' which is internal to the United States? One only has to read the work of Yvon Le Bot or Olga Odgers[7] to understand the importance of the border area between the United States and Mexico, where both sides of the border constitute an area in itself. We see to what extent the analysis implies a consideration of the two national entities together and even further afield.

France usually conceives of itself as a 'melting pot' and imagines that the immigrants who come there dream of living there. But, until it was closed by the French Ministry for the Interior, the problem represented by the Red Cross Centre in Sangatte, next to the entry for the tunnel under the Channel, revealed that numerous immigrants had only one idea, to leave France and go the United Kingdom and then perhaps elsewhere as Smain Laacher's excellent study shows.[8] Moreover, this model is based on an understanding of employment and work which does not entirely correspond to the reality; it cannot adequately deal with the phenomena of illegal employment, clandestine or subterranean immigration, which is either simply ignored, or criminalised.

Globalisation does not necessarily weaken nation states. But it does blur the borders between internal and external problems, between internal security and diplomacy or war, as we see with 'global' terrorism. Examples in recent years include its impact on the Spanish parliamentary elections and the attempt by the takers of French hostages in Iraq, to force France to abolish the recent law on 'conspicuous' religious emblems at school. Yet again, how can we, for example, understand contemporary anti-Semitism in France without referring to the Israeli–Palestinian conflict and the way in which it intervenes in French society, particularly as a result of the presence of Jewish, Arab and Muslim populations who may themselves feel to some extent directly concerned, if not involved.

There are two additional dimensions to this issue of globalisation. The first is that the nation states in Europe have initiated a process of

European construction which forces us to make the categories in which we think about these problems coherent. However, this is not obvious. Thus, for example, there is a gap between France which considers that the nation is defined by *ius solis*, and Germany where *ius sanguinis* is the principle, although Germany has distinctly reduced its scope in recent years. Yet again, British political culture will consider that discourse or practices which do not recognise ethnic or cultural minorities are racist, whereas in France, whenever discourse of this sort emerges, it is specifically described as racist. The second dimension which complicates the task of those who wish to define a territorial framework within which to consider cultural differences is the observation that the latter can be highly localised, at the level of a local area, or a town, with no reference to the national context, while not impeding those territorial frameworks that function at a transborder level. In the French suburbs, for example, one may well meet young people who do not know Paris, and who do not travel much in France but who regularly go to the distant country of origin of their parents.

The content of differences

In the 1970s and 1980s, discussions were dominated by one type of image of cultural differences: at the time, it was usually considered that each formed a whole which was relatively well delimited and which had a degree of stability, with a propensity to learn to coexist harmoniously with others. Was it not a question, as Alain Touraine famously argued, of living together with our differences?

But this image appears today as an oversimplification and we have to learn to add to it. The forceful return of the theme of the mixing or hybridisation of culture is one approach. This theme, of which there are fine examples in the work of Serge Gruzinski,[9] the historian of Mexico, has gained in importance, at least in a country like France, for reasons which are perhaps political. It does indeed present the dual politico-ideological advantage of enabling the discussion of cultural identities while at the same time promoting mixing or hybridisation and therefore the dissolution of minorities or constituted groups in a process of permanent recomposition and change to which there are no clearly defined limits or any sort of stability. The reference to hybridisation involves the recognition of the existence of processes of cultural innovation; we observe the existence of cultural actors but actors who have no propensity whatsoever to form groups or minorities which are likely to demand collective rights or a multiculturalist type of policy. In France, where the political model is republican, and therefore hostile to measures of recognition of cultural difference in the public sphere, it is easy to understand how the theme of hybridisation is well suited to the republican way of thinking, including in its hardest 'republicanist' variants. And symmetrically, in societies which are much more open to minorities and their rights, the theme of hybridisation is a way of resisting communitarianism, by appealing perhaps to a type of cosmopolitanism, or in any event, to universal values which hybridisation, by principle, cannot challenge. There are certainly other reasons for the rediscovery of hybridisation and similar themes such as creolisation and it has to be understood that this corresponds to observable realities: the fact remains that this phenomenon is now introducing an additional dimension to our thinking about differences.

A second dimension, to which we have already referred but to which we must return, has been emerging in an increasingly forceful way in recent years, and this is the concept of the subject. This concept, the importance of which in the work of the social sciences I have demonstrated elsewhere, can be placed at the very centre of the analysis in so far as it provides an instrument enabling us to consider invention and inventiveness, creativity and involvement: identities, work on the memory and identification with a culture, can no longer be understood today without taking into consideration the work that individuals do regarding themselves, the choices which they make, the capacity of each individual to be the subject of his or her experience, and also the acceptance of others and their potential as subjects. But this capacity can be exercised in various ways, and it can, moreover, also be hindered, or forbidden, for example as a result of racial discrimination or social exclusion. As mentioned already, it may result in an identification with a cultural difference or contribute to the production of collective identities (I choose to be Muslim); it may be at the core of an experience of hybridisation (I choose to be of mixed identity, to elaborate a syncretic culture which I invent in a process in which others invent other modes, continuing to ensure the process of mixing); it may also lead the actor to disengage himself from belonging to any specific identity, whether it be 'pure' or hybrid, and to assert him or herself as an individual with no attachments. There are therefore several possibilities and to summarise and simplify, we can distinguish five main types.

Culture and politics: five configurations

As the foregoing arguments suggest, we now have to envisage five main ways of configuring cultural difference. It is now possible to draw an axis which extends from the most structured identities to the total absence of individualist identity.

Five separate situations

In the first situation, cultural identity falls within the province of reproduction. I have already expressed my reservations about this concept because the identities which appeared to be the most deeply rooted in a remote past during which they were simply reproduced and resisted the processes which sought to undermine them, on closer examination, were in fact bearers of new elements. Let me give one example: Breton identity, as Ronan Le Coadic in his book demonstrates,[10] is an invention (the music is relatively recent and the architecture was borrowed from the Île-de-France two centuries ago); it is nevertheless often presented as particularly long-standing and traditional. But let us say that there are dimensions of reproduction, possibly on a large scale, in some identities. The main point here is that they call for a modus operandi in which there is hardly any room for the personal subject, because of the predominance of the law of the group and of those who embody authority. Identity here lies within the sphere of a 'holistic' analysis; it demands the adoption of the viewpoint of the totality and not that of the individual. There is a recurrent risk of members either wishing to cut themselves off from the rest of the world in an endeavour to ensure their perpetuation or, if there is a territorial dimension, desiring to break away or become autonomous; in any event, they never easily accept the values of the wider society within which they operate.

The second point on this axis is that of the collective identity which is relatively delimited and stabilised but which is very much alive and dynamic; here there is a recognition of the fact that identity is borne by processes of production or invention, capable of adapting to a wider society and has no difficulty in integrating into a democratic space. The outstanding feature here is that the group and the personal subject are complementary and not mutually destructive. There are countless variations here given the endless possibilities for combination or articulation involving varying degrees of tension between the universal and the particular and between the overall, individualist values of the society in question and the collective values of the minorities.

A third point on our axis represents the figure of the nomad, or the foreigner, in the meaning Georg Simmel gave the word,[11] explaining how the foreigner is not totally external to and distant from society but, at one and the same time, within and without, near and far. The nomad may belong to a strong, stable collective identity, be part of a diaspora, as is the case, for example, of the Roma when they become sedentary, which is increasingly the rule in Western Europe. Nomadism leaves a degree of latitude to the subjectivity of its members, and above all, it does not accept the framework of the nation state and its borders; nomadism may even at times pose a considerable challenge to those who wish to act politically by dealing with it in the strict framework of the nation state.

A fourth point is that of the cultural identity which is the outcome of mixing and which is, as a result, by definition unstable, and without defined limits; here identities do not form a group, or at best it is ephemeral (or if stabilised, is comparable to the preceding situation). In this case, the personal subject does not submit to the tensions which could bind it but also oppose it to the group. We should not deduce from this observation that hybridisation necessarily promotes the growth of creativity or resourcefulness of the subject; it may also, on the contrary, mould an impossible, or painful form of subjectivity, with a feeling of being at home nowhere and of not having any identity.

The last point is the one where the subject has no relation whatsoever to one or several cultural identities, is free of any attachment and has no links with a minority or a group. Creativity, resourcefulness, the construction of oneself as an actor of a culture is entirely up to the subject, and is consequently the most distant from the 'holism' mentioned above.

Obviously, these five types do not have the same relationship to policy, and it is on this point that we can begin to form our conclusions.

The move to policy

The question that must now be addressed is the following: what can the actors expect from policy regarding cultural identities? The actors who fall within the confines of reproduction wish their identity to be preserved, protected, to be uncontaminated by the outside world and possibly prosper and spread. They expect a policy either to grant them an autonomous status, even independence, to recognise the primacy of their own rules, or that they be granted specific cultural rights or at least toleration to enable the group to maintain strict control over its members, maintaining as high as possible a wall between the world within and the world without, to avoid their disintegration, which frequently begins with mixed marriages. In this case, the universal values of the rule of law and of reason may be flouted, starting with those which advocate equality between men and women. The liberty of the individual subjects is subordinated to the decisions of the group and its leaders. In this case, multiculturalism is totally inappropriate since it proposes to articulate universal values and specificities, whereas the actors see these as diametrically opposed and choose the latter rather than the former.

When there is a clearly defined collective identity which is relatively stable and open to personal subjectivity, the situation is totally different. Here it is possible to have a political and philosophical discussion to envisage one or other type of policy in response to demands. The two most realistic responses, and which deserve to be discussed, are tolerance and recognition: tolerance enables actors to live their difference, including in the public sphere, but under certain conditions, in particular in so far as they are not a source of trouble or disorder. Recognition suggests cultural rights. There are advantages and disadvantages to each of these two responses. A policy of tolerance means fragility for the existence of the groups targeted since the government can restrict it without having to provide any justification other than vague declarations concerning public order or national security. Those who are 'tolerated' are second-class citizens, or non-citizens who in periods of crisis or high tension live in fear of persecution. Moreover 'tolerance' discredits the culture of the minorities in question, if only because they are not allowed to be too visible in the public sphere. On the contrary, a policy of recognition can become a factor leading to processes of closure of identity. The cultural rights acquired may facilitate a drift towards processes of reproduction, exposing the members of the groups concerned, and society as a whole, to the dangers of communitarianism. Thus, two pitfalls threaten the political treatment of the processes of the collective production of identity. The first is the discrediting which tolerance may arouse; the second is the perversion whereby cultural rights, which at the outset were compatible with universal values, may give rise to the communitarianism which is their very negation.

Nomadism, the networks of the diaspora, and movements backwards and forwards in some cases pose problems which are comparable with the preceding situation: how can we implement a policy which respects the specificities of the actors while ensuring they respect universal values? But here, everything is complicated by the fact that we are dealing with transnational or transborder phenomena, which moreover may be unstable and may straddle several cultures or forms of national belonging. This in a way facilitates taking political decisions concerning them, for the latter are usually, or mainly, taken within the framework of a state. Everything concerning these differences may challenge simultaneously internal politics and policies and international politics and policies: for example, when France satisfies its Armenian communities by officially recognising the 1915 genocide, it creates diplomatic difficulties with Turkey. Or again: the first problem with the Muslim headscarf in 1989 was settled (and today this has been forgotten) not because of the behaviour of the French government, but because Hassan II, the King of Morocco, asked the young girls involved at the time, who were of Moroccan origin, to stop wearing the well-known 'veil' to school. Multiculturalism becomes inappropriate here as it then tends to destabilise the groups targeted by offering them recognition and rights which are part of institutions which are usually national, whereas these groups, even stable, need to be able to circulate and not to remain fixed. What would be the meaning of cultural rights which were only used occasionally, and are not deeply entrenched in the society which grants them?

Cultural hybridisation has nothing to expect from policies of collective recognition which are the complete opposite of its approach to change and mixing. A policy of this sort (multiculturalism), the granting of cultural rights, can only fix a process which to remain one of hybridisation must be able to change all the time. The actors of cultural hybridisation, and those who wish to encourage it, have nothing to gain in endeavouring to rise to the political level: they could only lose their souls. But, if hybridisation is to be totally operational, they require favourable political conditions. Society as a whole must be very open-minded, just as people are in their cultures of origin; there must be space for a high degree of communication and movement. A spirit of democracy is needed for the promotion of the hybridisation of cultures and creative forms of invention. But it is very much a question of enabling each person as an individual to construct themselves in the mixing of cultures; it is not a question of enabling groups to exist as such.

Finally, the personal subject, in so far as he or she has his or her own individuality with no attachments, requires political conditions which ensure their liberty far from any attachment to any form of identity which might take hold of them and make it difficult for them to control the expression and construction of their personal experience. For these people, multiculturalism is an obstacle or a brake because it promotes organised groups, and the individuals who belong to them, and gives nothing to the isolated individual.

These remarks would gain by being more specific. But even as they are, they enable us to make three political observations. The first is that there is not one problem of cultural difference but several, and that each type of cultural identity calls for discussions and policies distinct

from the others. The second observation is that the more cultural differences tend to be stable and to lie within the bounds of the nation state,
the more likely they are to demand rights, to plead for recognition in
the public sphere and to endeavour, on this basis, to benefit, directly or
not, from political representation. In other words, they are likely to participate in the interplay of representative democracy and at the very
least to question it. On the contrary, hybridisation does not give rise as
such to any possible form of political representation and this is all the
more true for the individualism of the subject without attachments.
This leads us to the third lesson which is that as the practice of individual subjectivity increases so does the tendency to turn it into a
central demand, prior to the recognition of a collective identity, if this
exists; this means that the actor increasingly expects from democracy
something other than simply the possibility of obtaining cultural
rights. In certain cases, this may lead to a desire to participate and
therefore to appeals for participatory democracy. But the main point is
that this means that the level of action, in cultural affairs, may have
nothing to do with the political level, in which case the actors do not
expect anything from the political system, apart from the very general
demands of liberty, equality or justice or, if you like, living conditions
which do not impose upon them any particular politicisation. This is
why, in France, cultural hybridisation may be used as an ideology in the
service of the values of the Republic and can be presented as a concili-
atory alternative to multiculturalism which then, even in a moderate
form, acts as a foil.

Finally, and to conclude by complicating things even further, we
should note that almost none of these remarks takes account of a very
real dimension which can only make the analysis even more complex.
Our identities are multiple and it may well be that the same person
belongs to two or more of the types which have been described, so
much so that they appear to be ambivalent or ambiguous, or yet again
beset by their own contradictions when they have to try to make a politically coherent statement.

Notes

1. A. Smith, *The Ethnical Revival in the Modern World* (Cambridge University
   Press: Cambridge, 1981).
2. G. Kepel, *La revanche de Dieu: chrétiens, juifs et musulmans à la reconquête du
   monde* (Paris: Le Seuil, 1990).
3. See, for example, C. Lévi-Strauss, *The Savage Mind* (London: Weidenfeld and
   Nicolson, 1974).

4. See, for example, the discussion of republican philosophy in R. Debray, *Que vive la République* (Paris: O. Jacob, 1989).
5. P. Gilroy, *The Black Atlantic: Modernity and Double Consciousness* (Cambridge, Mass.: Harvard University Press, 1993).
6. J.U. Ogbu, *Minority Education and Caste: the American System in Cross-cultural Perspective* (New York: Harcourt Brace Jovanovich, 1978).
7. O. Odgers, *Identités frontaltières: immigrés mexicains aux États-Unis* (Paris: L'Harmattan, 2001).
8. S. Laacher, *Après Sangatte: nouvelles immigrations, nouveaux enjeux* (Paris: La Dispute, 2002).
9. See, for example, S. Gruzinski, *La pensée métisse* (Paris: Fayard, 1999).
10. R. Le Coadic, *L'Identité bretonne* (Rennes: Presses universitaires de Rennes, 1998).
11. G. Simmel, 'The Stranger', in K.H. Wolff (ed.), *The Sociology of Georg Simmel* (New York: Free Press, 1950).

Select bibliography

Debray, R., *Que vive la République* (Paris: O. Jacob, 1989).
Gilroy, P., *The Black Atlantic: Modernity and Double Consciousness* (Cambridge, Mass.: Harvard University Press, 1993).
Gilroy, P., *Against Race: Imagining Political Culture beyond the Color Line* (Cambridge, Mass.: Harvard University Press, 2000).
Gruzinski, S., *La pensée métisse* (Paris: Fayard, 1999).
Kepel, G., *La revanche de Dieu: chrétiens, juifs et musulmans à la reconquête du monde* (Paris: Le Seuil, 1990).
Laacher, S., *Après Sangatte: nouvelles immigrations, nouveaux enjeux* (Paris: La Dispute, 2002).
Le Coadic, R., *L'Identité bretonne* (Rennes: Presses universitaires de Rennes, 1998).
Lévi-Strauss, C., *The Savage Mind* (London: Weidenfeld and Nicolson, 1974).
Odgers, O., *Identités frontaltières: immigrés mexicains aux États-Unis* (Paris: L'Harmattan, 2001).
Ogbu, J.U., *Minority Education and Caste: the American System in Cross-cultural Perspective* (New York: Harcourt Brace Jovanovich, 1978).
Smith, A., *The Ethnical Revival in the Modern World* (Cambridge University Press: Cambridge, 1981).
Wieviorka, M., *La différence culturelle: une reformulation des débats* (Paris: Balland, 2001).
Wolff, K.H. (ed.), *The Sociology of Georg Simmel* (New York: Free Press, 1950).

3
Debating Cultural Difference in France

Catherine Wihtol de Wenden

Introduction

France has a long tradition of state supremacy because it was centralised much earlier than other European states. This centralising policy took its roots in the effort by kings to fight against the diversities of their kingdom, which were also obstacles to the exercise of their strength. France is a multicultural country, which may be seen as a paradox given its typical image as a centralised and homogeneous country. France was made of many provinces with their own customs and their own rules. The French Revolution, the First and Second Empires, and the Third Republic went on reinforcing a unified state and republican ideology tried to impose the political myth of the citizen, defined by his/her political contract with the nation state, free and equal with regard to their rights, independent of any other sense of belonging.

The myth of national homogeneity and the indivisibility of the Third Republic lasted until new developments such as immigration, Europe and globalisation imposed other issues, such as multiculturalism and cultural difference, as new values. There has been a strong resistance to the call to recognise cultural difference, among the supporters of assimilation, republican values, the centralisation of the state, and those defenders of sovereignty and of a social contract comprised of rights and duties. This cleavage is less a left/right opposition than, on a scale of political behaviours, a conflict between authoritarians and liberals, citizenship 'à la française' versus diversities. In order to debate cultural diversities in France, we will first demonstrate how far cultural difference has always existed in France, even if it was sometimes hidden, and how it is now newly redefined with new debates around discrimination, identity and group loyalties.

Internal diversity, a long and controversial background within France

During the *Ancien Régime*, France was the most populated country in Europe (20 million under the reign of Louis XIV), with a highly diverse population. Although the compulsory use of the French language in the administration and the judiciary was introduced in 1539 (Edict of Villers Cotterêts), the defence and unification of French language took place in 1635 (creation of the French Academy by Richelieu) and the centralisation of public administration was accomplished in the seventeenth century (under the ethos of 'colbertisme' defined by the reforming civil servant Jean-Baptiste Colbert), France was divided into 'provinces' that had their own languages, their own taxes, tribunals, parliaments and systems of weights and measures. Due to the feudal society which gave birth to monarchy, some of them had preserved their feudal links with the kingdom (Brittany, Béarn, Provence), others were directly ruled by the state, while some had free or foreign allegiances (Alsace, Lorraine). France also included three bishoprics and a small kingdom, Navarre. These diversities introduced some discrepancies in the exercise of royal power on the eve of the revolution: some provinces expected their autonomy such as Brittany and Provence, Artois expected to be ruled by its own natives, the provincial parliaments were reluctant to abide by the king's law, and the population experienced difficulties in communicating and trading across the barriers created by various languages and customs rights. Most of these provinces had their own languages broadly separated by the *langue d'oil* in the north and *langue d'oc* in the south. As Mirabeau said during the revolution: 'Le royaume n'est encore qu'un agrégat de peuples désunis' (the kingdom is still but an aggregate of disunited peoples). But the revolution feared communities, groups, collective interests and promoted the individual citizen as the main actor in political life: the corporations of craftsmen were abolished in 1791 (Le Chapelier law) and the Jews were recognised as individuals but not as a community ('donnez aux juifs tous les droits en tant qu'individus mais aucun comme communauté'; 'give the Jews all rights as individuals but none as a community'), said Clermont Tonnerre in 1789. The revolution also promoted the birth of the French nation: 'Vive la Nation' was first used at the battle of Valmy in 1792. This was recognised by Goethe as the emergence of a new idea in Europe.

During the revolution, the pluralist and regionalist tendency, the Girondins, lost the battle against the centralising republicans, the

Jacobins. Some regions, such as the west (Vendée) or the south-east (Provence), rebelled against the revolution. These uprisings were brutally suppressed. The *départements* replaced the former provinces, which were dismantled in order to avoid communitarian rebel movements (the Catalans, for example, torn between the Hérault and the Pyrénées orientales). When Napoleon Bonaparte was crowned emperor, he reinforced and centralised the state, unified the laws (civil code in 1804 and penal code), a task which was continued by his nephew Napoleon III. But the defence of regional autonomy was still alive as a popular practice (regional dress, languages, local customs) and represented by Auguste Comte or Frédéric Le Play as a right-wing posture. The ideology of a homogeneous nation was mostly used during the Third Republic to mobilise the population in favour of the return to France of Alsace-Lorraine, lost in 1870 to Germany after defeat in the Franco-Prussian War. Thanks to some state-sponsored orchestration (statues, names of avenues, of squares, of republican celebrations such as the creation of 14 July as the national day), the republican symbol of 'Marianne' was opposed to that of 'Germania', presenting Germany as a people defined by their ethnicity. In 1871, Ernest Renan wrote his famous essay, *Qu'est-ce qu'une nation?*, in which he stressed the common heritage ('riche legs de souvenirs') and the sharing of common values ('vouloir vivre collectif') that united the French.

The ideology of the Third Republic went on to popularise the civic values of freedom, equality, fraternity and justice, thanks to educational reform (Jules Ferry's laws of 1882 and 1884 on compulsory, free and secular schooling) and to military service (compulsory for all in 1907), an enterprise of national amalgamation blurring internal borders and the differences developed. At school the children learned a newly written national and consensual history (recently written by Ernest Lavisse) and geography (mapped by Vidal de la Blache). A common image of France was shared thanks to the school book, *Le tour de France par deux enfants*, by Gaston Bruneau; the story of two young boys discovering France. The schoolmasters ('hussards noirs de la république', the 'black hussars of the republic') taught republican values as a set of moral and civic values. The access to public administration of those speaking and writing French was a factor of social promotion and the acceptance of republican values among a mostly rural population (75 per cent in 1914), which brought its adhesion to a centralised and jacobinist state. Local or regional 'cultures' were viewed as a factor of regression (it was prohibited to speak dialects at school), of social inequality and an obstacle to social promotion. The triumph of a meritocratic ideology was thought to be attainable due to the cultural neutrality of the school and the access it provided to a universal culture and language. But the unification of cultures was not so easy to achieve.

Some nostalgia for the former regions and cultures was still expressed: at the end of the nineteenth century, Frédéric Mistral tried to encourage the revival of the *langue d'oc* in Provence (the birth of his movement, Félibrige, was in 1876), and inspired the traditionalist Charles Maurras. Maurice Barrès transferred these particularistic identities to Lorraine, and later Jean Giono celebrated rurality and the local traditions of Provence in his novels. But it is during the Vichy regime, after the fall of France in 1940, that regionalist values acquired legitimacy in the state, against the centralisation and the republicanism embodied by Paris. Some regions which had a tradition of autonomy such as Alsace, Brittany and Provence favoured ethnic regionalisms with languages, cultures and traditions that became illegitimate due to their link with this period after the Second World War. A second revival was born out of the tumult of May 1968, which gave room to a leftist regionalism, expressed by Robert Laffont and some left-wing activists who professed a desire to go back to the countryside ('Vivre et travailler au pays'), to fight against Paris (such as the campaign mounted in 1974 to prevent the extension of an army base at Larzac, a geographical plateau in the south of France), and even against a form of globalised economy (the *altermondialiste* movement of environmentalist José Bové stresses the strengths of diversity and regionalism, and underlines the dangers of free-market globalisation). In the 1970s, the torch of regionalism passed from right to left. How was this swift transfer made possible? For a long time, the defence of the 'small' against the monolithic, centralised Parisian decision-making process was a very popular theme, used both by the radicals during the Third Republic, by the conservative populist party of Pierre Poujade in 1956, by the extreme right of Jean-Marie Le Pen and by the leftist rural movements of Confédération Paysanne, whose champion is José Bové. In that scenario, diversity meets various forms of communitarian solidarity that cohere in their opposition to the state and its centralised republican symbols.

Other particularisms continue to exist: in Corsica, the separatist fight goes on to challenge the state but the region has got its own parliament. Its language is taught in public schools and in the University, as is the case in Brittany, but the French Constitutional Council refused to recognise the existence of a 'Corsican people' in 1991, arguing that there is only a French people ('la Constitution ne reconnaît que le peuple français, composé de tous les citoyens français, sans distinction d'origine, de race ou de religion'; 'the constitution recognises only the French people, comprised of all French citizens, irrespective of origin, race or religion'). In Alsace, the German dialect can be used in local administration and in religious celebrations. In Catalan regions, the names of villages, streets and roads are written in the local and the national language, just like in Brittany, but France has not ratified the European Charter on regional and minority languages. In Alsace-Lorraine (the three departments of Haut-Rhin, Bas-Rhin and Moselle), the separation of Church and state, under legislation passed in 1905, is not applied because the region was under German rule during this period. They are still living under an agreement (the 'Concordat' of 1901) between the three religions (Protestant, Catholic and Jewish) and the state. Other exemptions are granted in the TOMS (overseas territories) to Muslim populations, for example polygamy is permitted in Mayotte, and in Vanuatu, the democratic elections there have to accommodate the existence of three kings. Such paradoxes are possible because those territories have special status, they benefit from the exceptionality derived from such distance from metropolitan France, their populations are mixed and demand respect for their specificity.

Moreover, contrary to many stereotypes, France is no longer a centralised country: the programme of decentralisation, launched in 1982, has introduced a lot of autonomy in management at regional level with more power and money. Under the pressure of tourism, of local voters attached to their regional identities, sometimes encouraged anew by traditional right-wing parties and with the revival of collective identities, internal diversities are introduced and celebrated on French territory (public and even religious festivities, open air markets, etc.). As the French are fond of history and genealogy and tourists are looking for rurality and traditions, in the summer most regions are celebrating their particularisms, customs, rural habits and cultural memories even if these identities are sometimes folkloric and in opposition to the national state (such as the *savoisien* movement in Savoy demanding more autonomy today) or fought strongly against it in the past (such as Cathars rebelling under the king and the Pope or the Protestants in Cévennes – the *camisards* – during the seventeenth century). However, new challenges emerged when France realised progressively that it was a country of settled immigration, rooted in Europe and in a globalised landscape.

External diversity, fuelled by immigration, Europe and globalisation

The struggle for recognition of external identities has been a long process because immigration has had difficulties in acquiring legitimacy. France is the oldest country of mass immigration in Europe but it long considered immigrants to be a short-term answer to labour shortages and not as future members of the national community. The emergence of a second generation in the late 1970s in the so-called *banlieues* or the outer suburbs of the major conurbations, set the themes of plural citizenship, cultural diversity inside the political discourse on nationality, citizenship and the political community. Other issues such as the emergence of Islam in Europe, multiple allegiances and anti-discrimination battles introduced debates on multiculturalism in France, a former taboo in the French republican model. The freedoms granted to foreign associations in 1981 gave the opportunity to immigrant associations to express new values of citizenship such as anti-racism and the 'right to difference' (the slogan of the association SOS Racisme, born in 1984), and also the 'right to indifference' for those 'visible' French who feel primarily French. Such claims for cultural pluralism had been encouraged for a long time beforehand by the Council of Europe, which argued for intercultural schooling and dialogue between cultures, equality between men and women in migration, and local political rights for foreigners.

But, under pressure from the far right National Front Party since 1983 and the first headscarf affair of 1989, the reaction of the political parties in power (left and right) has been to stress republican values: French identity (with books from the Club de l'Horloge like *Être Français, cela se mérite* in 1985 and from the socialist club Banlieues 89, *L'identité française*, in 1989)[1] has been defended by right and left. Citizenship and nationality were debated with the reform of the nationality code in 1993 and 1998, the social contract[2] and republican values have been reasserted in the criteria and conditions for integration (in the High Council on Integration reports, in the Sarkozy laws of 2003 and 2006 on the new policy of entry). Secularism has been debated from the headscarf affair of 1989 which led to jurisprudence from the Conseil d'Etat or State Council prohibiting 'ostentatious' Islamic veils in school, to the Commission on Secularism appointed in 2004 which has inspired a law prohibiting the wearing at school of all religious symbols if they are *ostensibles* (conspicuous). Some institutions such as the High Council on Integration have considered themselves as the guardians of republican values, stressing in their reports on rights and duties, the civic values of citizenship, religious neutrality and jacobinism.

However, some new topics, mostly brought by the *beur* movement, have been introduced in the debate:[3] plural citizenship, collective identities, dissociation between nationality and citizenship (the so-called 'new citizenship', established by participation in local life, here and now, independent of nationality, following the model promoted during the revolution in the Constitution of 1793, which gave French citizenship to those who deserved to be granted citizenship on account of their civic behaviour). While the young of visibly foreign origin stress their difference and alternative sense of belonging, in the population of French origin, a racialisation and ethnicisation of social relations has emerged reciprocally, with some people defining themselves as 'Français de souche',[4] which is contrary to the French ideology of the nation. They are developing a racism built on their own difference ('racisme différentialiste'). In the background, Islam has raised the question of double allegiances, dissent, the possible influence and intrusion of countries of origin in the case of votes for dual nationals, transnational networks, internal and external security. But many Islamic associations are struggling for a citizen's way of practising Islam at local level[5] and most of them want to be recognised as French and Muslims. There are approximately 5 million Muslims in France, although the censuses on religious affiliation have disappeared in France since 1872. Around half of them are French of the so-called 'second and third generations'. Others are of numerous countries: Algeria, Tunisia and Morocco principally, but also Turkey, Senegal, Mali, Mauritania, various Middle Eastern countries and Pakistan. Then there are the Harkis (the families of those Algerians who fought on the French side during the war of independence and who were repatriated to France after 1962), and finally there are the French who have converted to Islam.

Of the 1500 places of Muslim worship in France counted in 1999, there are eight big mosques with prayer rooms capable of welcoming more than 1000 people, and they are trying to come to terms with a republican discourse. The most famous of them is the big mosque in Paris, built in 1926 to thank the Muslim soldiers of the First World War for their sacrifices at Verdun. The rector there, Dalil Boubaker, has dual citizenship, French and Algerian, was appointed by Algeria, and is very respectful of French jacobinist values of secularism. He is the head of the CFCM (Conseil français du culte musulman), a structure for facilitating dialogue, created by the Interior Minister in 2003 with a mission to address the questions raised by Islam in the public space (hallal meat markets, slaughtering of livestock, the wearing of veils, conflicts with the law) and recognises Islam as a religion of France. In emblematic institutions such as the army and the police, the will to mirror the image of the nation with the recruitment of 'second generation' minorities is also a concern, even if the inclusion of those newcomers may create some clash with the subculture of some French citizens in those places where the memory of the Algerian war, the presence of extreme right-wing activists and a tolerance of discrimination may subsist. Most French people do not consider that those citizens whose difference is 'visible' are totally French, which leads to an ethnicised practice of relations with the new French in everyday life: identity controls in the streets, institutionalised racism in relations with institutions of authority, amalgamations of them as homogeneous groups, refusing opportunities to individuals as a result of group stereotyping.

Recently, immigration has acquired more legitimacy with the celebration of its memory in French history: a Museum of the History and Memory of Immigration (Cité Nationale de l'Histoire de l'Immigration) was due to open (opening now scheduled for July 2007) in Paris, under the auspices of the former Minister of Culture, Jacques Toubon, a close associate of former President Jacques Chirac. Reconciling immigration with French history, he writes: 'Since the beginning of the nineteenth century, France has been a great country of immigration. This continued process has contributed to the building of the nation.'[6] Located in the beautiful former colonial museum of Porte Dorée Palace near Vincennes in Paris, opened by Lyautey during the colonial exhibition of 1931, the ethos of the new museum is that 'their history is our history', which tries to give legitimacy to the contribution of immigration to the French population and the collective memory. The Arab language has been officially taught in some public schools since the beginning of the twentieth century, and in French universities. In the meantime, the Berber language spoken by several Berber groups such as the Kabyles of Algeria and the Moroccans from the Rif in the north and from the south (Agadir) has also been recognised as a language of France.

Moreover, immigration has changed the content of citizenship by the introduction of new values absent from the former definition of civic values in the Declaration of Human Rights of 1789, and put the emphasis on the implementation of rights. Some of them are even contrary to the French philosophy consisting in asserting rights more than controlling the feasibility of the access to these rights. Anti-discrimination has been introduced by two laws, implementing article 13 of the Amsterdam treaty, voted in 2001 and 2002. They are mainly focused on discrimination at work and in public places, but they do not solve the very difficult question of police discrimination towards the young, a question which was at the centre of the riots of November 2005. In 2003, a High Authority for the Fight against Discrimination and for Equality (HALDE) was appointed by the government, headed by a senior civil servant, Jean-Louis Schweizer.

Since 2005, the theme of positive discrimination has been introduced by Nicolas Sarkozy, including the mention of origins in French statistics. But positive discrimination has, since the *beur* period of the mid-1980s, been an unspoken practice in associations and municipal councils, which has helped the emergence of a middle class of immigrant origin without, however, helping others to escape from territorial exclusion in inner cities, housing, school and employment. A strong dependence on territories, due to the territorialisation of public policies (for example urban and educational) leads to an ethnicisation of poverty. But many lawyers, along with the CNCDH (Commission Nationale Consultative des Droits de l'Homme) and the CNIL (Commission Nationale de l'Informatique et des Libertés) consider that the mention of loyalties and origins, as well as positive discrimination policies, are contrary to the republican values of citizenship. Some people of Maghreb origin have been appointed in the government as secretaries of state (Tokia Saïfi in 2002 and Azouz Begag in 2005), including a so-called 'Muslim' prefect and a Muslim rector (head of an Academy) and some cabinet members. In most cases, the use of the word 'Muslim' does not mean they practise Islam but that they are 'of Arab and colonial origin', which is unbelievable in French discourse. Positive discrimination has been more successful in the headquarters of some political parties (Socialist, Green) and large associations (such as SOS Racisme, and MRAP, i.e. Mouvement contre le Racisme et pour l'Amitié entre les Peuples). But there are no deputies except in the European Parliament, and local councillors in the municipalities are mostly confined to dealing with migration and integration 'problems'.

Such a situation is not without ambiguities: some forms of neo-colonial management can be seen, namely at local level, where diversity exists in the consciousness of public elites rather than in the practices of people working on the ground. Since the mid-1980s, leaders of associations and local elites from the 'communities' have been appointed as cultural mediators, people at the cutting edge expressing both universal civic and ethnic group values. They have to play the multicultural game of helping the French and immigrants to live together and to fight against violence in urban areas ('vivre ensemble'), exercising the power delegated to them by the municipalities for the administration of urban policy, and in so doing running the risk of becoming 'arabes de service' (token Arabs). They are viewed as the symbols of multiculturalism because of their fidelity to republican values, sometimes more than most French people. They 'set the tone' in French integration policy, due to the long and passionate colonial relations between France and these groups who are very familiar with the rules of the game, managing republican and community values in a way that is shaped by the colonial past. No other group, Chinese, Turkish, sub-Saharan African, Italian, Polish or Portuguese, can negotiate diversity in the French state as they do. But other associations are demanding a more neutral position such as 'The indigenous peoples of the Republic' and the black organisations (Conseil Représentatif des Associations Noires) who denounce the manner in which the perception of immigration issues is coloured by France's colonial heritage. For electoral reasons, minority communities have become a focus of political concern. The recent vote, in 2006, of a law condemning the Armenian genocide, proposed by the right-wing MP Patrick Devedjian and strongly criticised by the Turkish embassy in Paris, was considered to be a turning point in the ethnicisation of politics and the definition of official memory by politicians in France.

Apart from immigration, Europe, by virture of its definition of a European citizenship that is decoupled from nationality, has introduced the possibility of plural allegiances inside citizenship. Many regional loyalties have also been made possible thanks to Europe, when the nation state was reluctant to accommodate them, such as with the recognition of Catalonia. One can now be a national, a European and a citizen of a local community, while having collective allegiances, ethnically and culturally. But these loyalties do not have the same intensity: the manner in which one can feel European is different from the manner in which one feels oneself a member of a nation or a community.[7] The transnational demand for the recognition of cultural difference is also more easily heard at European level than in France, but the reality and visibility of the changes that have occurred help its recognition.

Globalisation opens the way to a vast and multicultural city and the kind of citizenship that challenges French values. We are far from a citizenship shaped by migration, such as in Canada or in Australia.[8] The result in these countries which have been defined by mass immigration is the emergence of a multicultural democracy. Even if, in France, multicultural differences are not equal and meet diverse institutional responses, even if the state is not neutral when it regulates cultural identities, multiculturalism in France is negotiated with immigrants and minority practices. There is a reciprocal instrumentalisation of immigration and of multiculturalism as tools for a plural and global society in the process of being formed.

Notes

1. Espaces 89, *L'identité française* (Paris: Editions Tierce, 1985).
2. D. Schnapper, *La communauté des citoyens* (Paris: Gallimard, 1996).
3. C. Wihtol de Wenden and R. Leveau, *La beurgeoisie. Les trois âges de la vie associative issue de l'immigration* (Paris: CNRS Editions, 2001).
4. M. Wieviorka, *Une société fragmentée. Le multiculturalisme en débat* (Paris: La Découverte, 1996).
5. J. Cesari and C. Wihtol de Wenden (eds), 'Musulmans d'Europe', CEMOTI, no. 33 (2002).
6. J. Toubon, *Mission de préfiguration du Centre de ressources et de mémoire de l'immigration. Rapport au premier Ministre* (Paris: La Documentation française, 2004).
7. C. Wihtol de Wenden, *La citoyenneté européenne* (Paris: Presses de Sciences Po, 1997). See also E. Balibar, *We, the People of Europe. Reflections on Transnational Citizenship* (Princeton: Princeton University Press, 2004).
8. S. Castles and A. Davidson, *Citizenship and Migration. Globalization and the Politics of Belonging* (Basingstoke: Palgrave Macmillan, 2000).

Select bibliography

Bertossi, C. (ed.), *European Anti-discrimination and the Politics of Citizenship. Britain and France* (Basingstoke: Palgrave Macmillan, 2007).

Bertossi, C. and Wihtol de Wenden, C., *Les couleurs du drapeau. Les militaires français issus de l'immigration* (Paris: Robert Laffont, 2007).

Body-Gendrot, S. and Wihtol de Wenden, C., *Police et discriminations. Le tabou français* (Paris: L'Atelier, 2003).

Brouard, S. and Tiberj, V., *Français comme les autres* (Paris: Presses de Sciences-Po, 2005).

Héran, F., *Le temps des immigrés* (Paris: Seuil, 2007).

Mohammed, A. (ed.), *Histoire de l'islam et des musulmans en France du Moyen Age à nos jours* (Paris: Albin Michel, 2006).

Rex, R., *Ethnicité et citoyenneté. La sociologie de sociétés multiculturelles* (Paris: L'Harmattan, 2006).

Rex, R. and Singh, G. (eds), *Governance in Multicultural Societies* (Aldershot: Ashgate, 2004).

Sellam, S., *La France et ses musulmans. Un siècle de politique musulmane 1895–2005* (Paris: Fayard, 2006).

Vasta, E. and Vuddamalay, V., *International Migration and the Social Sciences. Confronting National Experiences in Australia, France and Germany* (Basingstoke: Palgrave Macmillan, 2006).

Weil, P., *La république et sa diversité. Immigration, intégration, discriminations* (Paris: Seuil, 2005).

4
The French Republic Unveiled[1]

Max Silverman

Introduction: beards, headscarves ... and other offensive weapons

In the Marx Brothers' classic film, *A Day at the Races*, Groucho taunts his habitual rival, Herman Gottlieb, with the comment 'Don't point that beard at me – it might go off.' This is not so far-fetched. In the debate on the ban on ostentatious signs of religious affiliation in French schools in 2004,[2] it was suggested by the French Education Minister, Luc Ferry, that beards of a certain length and worn in a particular way could indeed be a weapon, admittedly a cultural/political weapon rather than a piece of deadly hardware but no less dangerous for that. Worn by a Muslim and interpreted by the state as a sign of religious affiliation (and, as such, breaching the long-standing secular code of French schooling, i.e. *laïcité*) the beard could signal a challenge to the very principles of the Republic, despite the fact that Jules Ferry, Clemenceau and other giants of the French Third Republic sported, apparently unashamedly, an abundance of facial hair. As David Macey notes ironically, Jules Ferry's beard 'was presumably a republican beard'.[3]

France is clearly not the only Western country to fear the Muslim beard. In the police raid on a suspected terrorist house in Forest Gate, London on 2 June 2006, Mohammed Abdul Kayar, who was shot and wounded by the police, stated, 'The only crime I have committed is being Asian and having a long length beard.'[4] How long can a beard be before it becomes a political weapon? How can one distinguish between a discreet and ostentatious deployment of signs of cultural difference? What signs of cultural identity are acceptable in the public sphere? At the time of the French debate on this issue, when, as is well known, the Islamic headscarf was the object deemed most offensive to secular eyes, there were contradictory answers to these questions. For example, while his government was reinforcing the ban on headscarves in schools to protect the neutrality of the public sphere from the threat of cultural diversity, Jacques Chirac was lobbying UNESCO to support a worldwide charter to protect cultural diversity in an attempt to safeguard the French language and cinema from the global dominance of American English and the Hollywood blockbuster.

However, once again it would be wrong to suggest that it is only in France that such contradictions occur over the question of diversity in the public sphere. Shortly after supporters of multiculturalism in Britain had condemned France for its illiberal ban on headscarves, Britain was faced with its own variation of the headscarf affair. First, in June 2004, a 15-year-old Muslim girl in Luton, Shabina Begum, decided (or was it decided for her?) to come to school wearing a *jilbab* (the Muslim full-length headed gown). For some of those in Britain who had actually supported the right of French Muslim girls to wear their headscarves, this particular display was a bridge too far and they supported the judge's decision to uphold the school's ban of the *jilbab* (a decision which was overturned on appeal, and then subsequently reinstated). Following this, comments by Jack Straw on his preference for Muslim women to unveil for purposes of communication when consulting him in his Blackburn constituency, and the dismissal of the teaching assistant Aishah Azmi from a school in Dewsbury, West Yorkshire, for refusing to remove her veil in class, brought the whole question to the top of the political agenda in Britain. Although it is generally the full veil that it is at issue in Britain (the *naqib*) and the headscarf in France (the *hidjab* or *tchador*), and despite the constant confusion of these and other terms, the more significant questions of which these developments are symptomatic are often the same, which, put crudely and schematically in the way they often appear in the media, can be reduced to similarity and difference, integration and multiculturalism.

Confusion and contradiction surrounding signs of cultural difference are, thus, clearly not confined to any single country. This is especially the case in a climate of ever-accelerating transnational and globalising cultural and political processes. However, the fact that signs cannot be contained within a national context does not necessarily mean that their interpretation is not still dependent, to a certain extent, on a national story. In this chapter I will first argue that France continues to 'veil' itself in a mythical past concerning the Republic and race. I will then argue that contemporary debates about the visibility of signs of cultural difference in the public sphere often reproduce this mythologised view of the French Republic. Finally I will suggest that there is a need to demythologise republican memory and expose the hidden mechanism of the republican model for a proper understanding of the present. Although understanding the past does not automatically guarantee a problem-free future, it is fairly safe to say that a mythologised past invariably reduces the possibility of any understanding at all. This chapter is not about the headscarf, the beard or any other sign of cultural difference per se but, by reversing the gaze on republican France, attempts to unveil the hidden ideology of the French republican model which constructs headscarves and beards as political weapons.

Paradoxes of the republican model

In his writings on Jews in modern France, the historian Shmuel Trigano points up the essential paradox of Enlightenment universalism. He demonstrates how the attempt to strip the Jew of his attachment to a collectivity and convert him into a citizen (as part of the process of emancipation) reinforces the very collectivity that the process is set against dissolving. In other words, by attempting to convert the other into the same, the boundaries of the other are, paradoxically, fixed ever more firmly.[5] Hence, the very fact that the Jew must undergo the process of transformation and assimilation in order to become a citizen (or 'regeneration' as it was termed at the time of the emancipation of the Jews just after the French Revolution) is a permanent reminder of the essential difference between Jews and 'natural' Frenchmen and women in the first place: the former will always be 'acculturated' (and hence duplicitous, mimics) compared to the latter, for whom culture and mores do not have to be acquired but are as much a part of their make-up as their very own skin. Trigano puts it thus:

> At the dawn of modern France, a process was thus set in motion that eventually led to the collectivization of the Jews – despite the fact that such a phenomenon was ruled out by the logic of the one and indivisible Republic. This irrepressible tendency of the republican system to turn the Jews into the very entity that the system forbade them to become could be likened to the psychoanalytic logic of the return of the repressed.[6]

Though Trigano's thesis concerns the situation of the Jew under conditions of modernity, it could be generalised to explain a fundamental paradox concerning the French republican model of the nation and the question of cultural/racial difference.[7] Trigano's use of the psychoanalytic notion of the 'return of the repressed' elucidates the way in which the disavowal of difference on the conscious level is premised on the fetishisation of difference on an unconscious level.[8] The splitting and Manichaean boundary-drawing at the heart of this Enlightenment model (dependent on the now familiar binary oppositions between universalism and particularism, assimilation and difference, citizen and subject, civilisation and barbarity, secularism and faith, public and private, individual and collectivity, and so on) ensures that any ambivalence remains firmly repressed and displaced. On the other hand, the victims of this double bind, whose difference is both denied and fetishised at the same time, are fully immersed in this modern ambivalence.[9] Jean-Paul Sartre's classic exposé of the situation of the Jew in his 1946 text *Anti-Semite and Jew*,[10] though flawed in many ways, is still a powerful reminder of the trap for the Jew set by the universalist democrat who offers the Jew an invitation to join humanity on the condition that he erases the stigma of his Jewishness.[11] Frantz Fanon's *Black Skin, White Masks*, indebted in great part to Sartre's text, reveals the same trick played on the black in the colonial context and unmasks the objectifying, racialising, essentialising and dehumanising gaze at the heart of French universalism. In his preface to Fanon's *The Wretched of the Earth*, Sartre describes this as 'a racist humanism since the European has only been able to become a man through creating slaves and monsters'.[12] The Republic does not recognise race and yet, through a process of disavowal, fetishisation and projection, politicises and racialises self and other in a most profound way so that the other becomes 'the repository of (our) repressed fantasies'.[13] The problem with contemporary debates in republican France, even after decades of postcolonial and postmodern questioning of Western universalism, is that the pillars of this fantasy are still firmly in place.

If Trigano is correct that the above process is an 'irrepressible tendency of the republican system', the lesson of republican history is that it is a tendency that is still largely unacknowledged. 'Race' was not banished with the call for equality and liberty (as many republicans would have us believe) but, from the outset, was built into the very fabric of the republican nation and returns in distorted form today, particularly in debates on immigration, headscarves, the suburbs (*la banlieue*), national identity and so on. In her remarkable post-war work, *The Origins of Totalitarianism*, Hannah Arendt makes what appears to be an exaggerated claim that 'the representatives of the great nations knew only too well that minorities within nation-states must sooner or later be either assimilated or liquidated'.[14] The progressive nationalisation of the home community during the second part of the nineteenth century, and especially the legalisation of the boundaries of the nation in relation to those who were subsequently defined as stateless and illegal people, did not in itself signal the onset of totalitarianism. However, by highlighting the accelerating racialisation of the nation from the end of the nineteenth century, Arendt's argument demonstrates that, rather than being a formation totally alien to parliamentary regimes, totalitarianism was instead an offshoot of incipient tendencies within the nation state, 'perplexities', as Arendt says, which even date back to the Rights of Man, where the human (universal) and the national were already confused.[15] Ruling in the name of a sovereign people, hence leaving unprotected those who are deemed outside the boundaries of the nation, was not simply the invention of totalitarian rulers guided by the principle of race but profoundly inscribed within the nation state of the nineteenth century.

Arendt demystifies and demythologises 'race' and shows how it emerges within, not outside, the structures of the parliamentary nation state. Yet conventional wisdom in France (and often in Britain as well) on models of the nation presents an opposition between the ethnic or racial model and the political or contractual model, which is often portrayed as the same opposition between the republican universalism of the French Enlightenment and the ethnic or racial particularism of German romanticism based on the concept of the 'Volk'.[16] However, the process of cultural homogeneity enforced through the institutions of the nation state in the latter part of the nineteenth century could breed imagined communities or, in the words of Étienne Balibar, 'fictive ethnicities' every bit as exclusive as those movements founded on more overtly racial models of the nation. Arendt's analysis shows how the political model and the ethnic/racial model of the nation are not opposites but profoundly imbricated.[17] Using the psychoanalytic terms above, the proclaimed race-free depiction of (French) Enlightenment universalism is premised on a disavowal of its own fetishised racial ambivalence and projection of it onto the (German) romantic tradition of race.

Though largely unacknowledged, this particular paradox of French republicanism has received a degree of critical attention in recent years. Etienne Balibar has consistently highlighted the historical articulations rather than oppositions between race and nation,[18] while Jean-Loup Amselle notes that 'at the heart of republican assimilation (...) lies a raciological principle'.[19] Yet, as Sue Peabody and Tyler Stovall rightly point out, '(m)any scholars in France have been curiously resistant to any discussion of race as a factor in national life'.[20] There has been even more resistance to any discussion of similar connections between the Republic and Empire. Fanon is hardly discussed in France (and when he is, 'the readings are negative').[21] Yet his indictment of a Manichaean racialised order at the heart of French universalism has lost none of its persuasive force. In that same post-war moment, Arendt's work too analyses the connections between empire-building outside Europe and racial politics inside Europe. The power of the republican myth has meant that France has been slow to re-evaluate these connections, so that in their groundbreaking work on this issue, Nicolas Bancel, Pascal Blanchard and Françoise Vergès can justifiably claim that 'the centrality of a racial division, of imaginary frontiers of the nation which are articulated with (invented) racial frontiers is simply not questioned'.[22] They demonstrate how, in the context of the colonies, 'the inequality of races' and 'republican principles' are not at all incompatible: the link is simply disguised by what they call 'the double discourse of republican law'[23] (and what Patrick Weil, playing with Michel Foucault's title *Les Mots et les choses*, has described as 'the confusion between the words of the law and the thing-ness of lived experience'.[24]

Unveiling the paradoxes of the republican model is not simply a question of pointing up contradictions or revealing hypocrisy, such as the republican use of an egalitarian rhetoric at home while racialising and subjugating others in the colonies, the use of ethnic criteria in a supposedly 'race-free' immigration policy and theories of a 'threshold of tolerance' in a supposedly 'race-free' housing policy, and so on. This suggests two opposing practices brought together in contradictory fashion, and also a conscious and instrumentalist exploitation of racial categories behind the façade of a race-free republic. But, as Gary Wilder rightly points out, the republican nation state and colonial ambitions are part of the *same* process (which he terms 'the imperial nation state'): 'a (cultural) racism that was simultaneously universalizing and particularizing (...) operate(d) within rather than against a republican framework'.[25] In his recent study of the Algerian War, Todd Shepard makes a similar point: the (fictional) rewriting of decolonisation by French officials at the moment of Algerian independence in 1962 as the logical outcome of colonialism and of France's historic mission towards progress removes blame from the French Republic and, conveniently, 'avoid(s) grappling with questions of "racial" or "ethnic" difference, or with racism'.[26] These studies show how republicanism speaks with two tongues at the same time, the second one often operating at the unconscious level through the discourse on the nation. Constructed on the building-blocks of universalism, *laïcité*, citizenship and assimilation, the republican model disavows its own role in racialising self and other and, through this Enlightenment sleight of hand, presents itself as the neutral opponent of all particular identities in the public sphere. Unveiling the historical foundations of the republican model may allow us to reinterpret contemporary debates on signs of cultural difference.

Visible differences

As all republicans know, a major function of the French state is to preserve the public sphere as a space of uniformity, neutrality and equality, consigning differences to the private sphere. The Republic therefore operates on a colour-blind basis. As Nordmann and Vidal point out, the French state has traditionally practised 'a policy of invisibility'.[27] However, if the presence of race within the structures of the Republic has been conjured away, as I have suggested above, then this 'policy of invisibility' needs to be reassessed. Paul Gilroy observes that '(w)hen it comes to the visualization of discrete racial groups, a great deal of fine-tuning has been required'.[28] In his essay on 'Racism and Culture', Fanon calls the subterfuge of race in liberal discourse 'a verbal mystification'.[29] The very fact that beards, headscarves and so on can provoke a national crisis may be symptomatic of the return of the repressed, of this 'fine-tuning' and 'verbal mystification' in contemporary France.

The unconscious effects of the republican model, as outlined by Trigano regarding the Jew or Bancel et al. regarding colonialism, are paradoxically an accentuation of the perception of difference rather than making differences invisible. By disavowing the other's difference while at the same time fetishising it through racialisation or exoticisation (thus declaring implicitly that you can and you cannot be like us, you are both same and different at one and the same time), the republican model politicises difference while proclaiming the opposite. And the more the state attempts to police the boundaries between public (universalist) and private (particularist) spheres, the sharper the public perception of difference becomes. As Zygmunt Bauman says:

> *The rule precedes reality.* Legislation precedes the ontology of the human world. The law is a design, a blueprint for a clearly circumscribed, legibly marked, mapped and signposted habitat. It is the law that brings lawlessness into being by drawing the line dividing the inside from the outside.[30]

Laws of uniformity politicise, and often pathologise, what might not have been political signs beforehand. Consequently, in a climate of boundary-policing, headscarves and beards can be instantly politicised whatever their initial intention. The ultimate paradox of the republican model is therefore that it politicises certain differences (considered unacceptable in the public sphere) while depoliticising others (considered 'neutral' and 'value-free') and then turns this process on its head by maintaining that it is those who insist on flaunting their differences in the public sphere who are politicising and endangering the neutrality of that space.

If this is accurate then the ways in which French republicans habitually demonise the American and British model for institutionalising differences could be reinterpreted as the disavowed ambivalence over racialised difference, inherent in the republican system, projected onto a 'foreign' system which explicitly recognises difference. If the disavowal and projection of race onto the German romantic tradition characterised the modern era, the postmodern era swaps the demon of the *Volksgeist* for that of the 'Anglo-Saxon' tradition of multiculturalism.[31] Now the republican fear is social division according to community or ethnic attachment, the development of 'American-style' ghettos, segregation and even soft forms of apartheid. Françoise Gaspard and Farhad Khosrokhavar define this fear as 'the fragmentation of French society into religious or ethnic "communities", closed in on themselves and potentially antagonistic and consequently a threat to national cohesion'.[32]

Yet any cursory glance at immigration policy and social processes in France since 1945 reveals that what is projected as an 'Anglo-Saxon' disease is, in reality, profoundly inscribed in the French social and national landscape, first in the form of *bidonvilles* (shanty towns) outside the major cities, then in the suburbs of those same cities, in which an ethnic or religious underclass has become divided from mainstream French society. Forms of racialised segregation are not absent from French national life but the role of race in social stratification is, once again, rarely acknowledged.[33] Consequently, where racialization is a de facto part of everyday life, no effective policy or practice can be put in place to address the situation because, *de jure*, racial categories are profoundly disavowed. At its worst, the republican model creates the beast but dare not speak its name.

In the light of the above, we might reconsider whether differences are more visible in a more pluralist and multicultural public sphere, like that of Britain, or in a more rigidly uniform public sphere like that of France. Although it would seem to be logical that pluralism recognises differences, while the insistence on uniformity suppresses differences, it could actually be the case that differences are rendered more, not less, visible in homogenising states. In other words, the more the state insists on uniformity and the neutrality of the public sphere, paradoxically the more it renders visible the very differences it wishes to erase; the more it insists on invisibility, the more it constructs the visibility of particular differences. At a time when racism focuses especially on the surface signs of cultural difference (headscarves, beards, odours, synagogues, gravestones and so on), one has to question the role of the republican state in fostering a climate in which signs of difference are stigmatised and outlawed.

Paradoxically, then, France's republican-inspired boundary-policing approach to cultural difference in the public sphere arguably produces a more profound fetishisation and racialisation of expressions of difference and cultural identity today than those states in which race is institutionalised. The explosion of sociological literature on identity in recent years has highlighted the ways in which ethnic and cultural signs are frequently manipulated today not as markers of racial belonging but as symbolic markers of identity.[34] These signs may be fleeting proclamations of a shifting identity rather than organic manifestations of an essential self and a homogeneous community. By attaching monolithic political motives to what might be a playful postmodern approach to identity and ethnicity (even a fashion statement), the French state is seriously misreading contemporary urban youth culture and contributing to its racialisation. By seeing in every headscarf or beard a potential threat to secularised, Western civilisation, French republicans are often unable to see a more complex picture in which the playful and symbolic deployment of cultural/ethnic signs for some, as a fundamental part of what Said Bouamama has called the 'contemporary need for identity',[35] coexists with the need by others to root those signs in a cultural tradition. The desire for difference and a fear of ceaseless difference are the twin markers today of an age of rootlessness in which signs are less and less bound organically to a community and increasingly part of the individual drama of recognition.[36]

Furthermore, the boundary-policing approach to the visibility of cultural difference is also a distraction from other threats. The energy, passion and resources deployed to regulate the question of visibility are in inverse proportion to the ability to control the real forces which determine lives today. As Zygmunt Bauman points out, these are global and are largely outside the control of any national law:

> Uncertainty and anguish born of uncertainty are globalization's staple products. State powers can do next to nothing to placate, let alone quash uncertainty. The most they can do is to refocus it on objects within reach; shift it from the objects they can do nothing about to those they can at least make a show of being able to handle and control. Refugees, asylum seekers, immigrants – the waste products of globalization – fit the bill perfectly. [37]

The accompanying paradox is that France has become more intent on drawing boundaries and reinforcing punitive rules for failure to conform at the very time that boundaries have broken down under the weight of new global flows of commodities, communications and cultures (although France is by no means alone in this). Regulation at home goes hand in hand with deregulation in the international arena. Having lost its historical mission to forge a common culture (which it pursued in messianic fashion, largely through the developing institutions of the nation state in the latter part of the nineteenth century), France can hardly regiment its population today in the same way as in the past and indulge in the same cultural crusade. The regulation of cultural difference in the public sphere is really a symbolic, and largely superfluous, sideshow concealing far more serious problems about the French nation state in a postmodern and postcolonial era.

Republican memory

It took France over 25 years to revise myths of collaboration and resistance during the war and equally as long to reopen the account on the Algerian war of independence (even for it to be named a 'war').[38] The process of 'decolonising mentalities'[39] is not always easy. However, the fact that France has been able to revisit its national stories about the past at least demonstrates an ability to confront difficult truths, no matter how divisive this can be. Perhaps the confrontation with some uncomfortable truths about the republican model is the final (and most difficult?) confrontation of them all as part of France's ongoing 'duty of memory'.[40]

Alain Touraine warns of the dangers of not doing this:

> those who adopt a defensive position lose all possibility of creating a new space for freedom. In the name of the Republic, they limit the

realm of democracy; in the name of traditional norms, they become incapable of recognising new rights, of creating new spaces for freedom and even of giving a new meaning to the national space. [41]

Touraine is suggesting that it is precisely an ossified and mythologised version of the Republic that stands in the way of a new democratic politics. To present equality and difference, equality and freedom, integration and multiculturalism as opposites (a familiar weapon in the republican armoury for attacking the rise of democratic freedoms based on identity and community) is both a misleading and outdated dichotomy.[42] Deeply rooted in the Enlightenment binary opposition between universalism and particularism, this memory of the Republic continues to disavow its own ambivalence around race and its own part in the construction of visible differences.[43]

The danger of not confronting the connections and echoes between the Republic and its others is that (particular) cultural identities will continue to be considered antithetical to national belonging, national identity and (most seriously of all) national security. This plays into the hands of racist organisations like the Front National whose political capital derives more or less exclusively from the implicit assumption that national belonging depends on cultural belonging. As the journalist Gary Younge points out, traditional republican rhetoric offers a loaded choice to minorities, 'convert or be damned': 'Faced with a nation where one-fifth of the electorate vote fascist and the state wants your headscarf, some young French Muslims may well end up in the arms of a misogynous imam.'[44] Stigmatising differences according to the principles of the secular Left at the time of the Dreyfus Affair today risks alienating the very people to whom any new democratic project must base its appeal.

Conclusion

Unreconstructed republican memory rests on an anachronistic vision of social life, dependent on boundaries constructed in the modern era which, in an age of deterritorialised and hybridised identities, are shown to be wanting. However, as is frequently the case, rhetorical principles and doctrinaire official discourse based on a mythologised past are out of step with realities on the ground. As the French sociologist François Dubet says in relation to the school, 'practices are more flexible and moderated than principles and those who criticize the rigours of a national republican universalism are referring more to Jules Ferry than the practices of teachers themselves'.[45] Republicanism is not a mono-lithic block and contemporary actors subvert the rigidity of outmoded structures in all sorts of ways.[46] Perhaps it is now time for the outworn rhetoric and mythologised national memories to catch up with the more nuanced practice.

The first chapter of Frantz Fanon's book on the Algerian war of inde-pendence, *A Dying Colonialism*, is entitled 'Algeria unveiled'. It explores the psychosexual drives which propel the male coloniser's desire to see beyond the Algerian woman's veil. Fanon attempts to unveil the colo-nising look of the French Republic (and its accompanying fantasies) in *its* attempt to unveil Algeria, just as Edward Said would do two decades later in his pioneering work on Orientalism. 'Decolonising mentalities', central to the projects of Fanon and Said, has still not run its course. A more complete unveiling of the Republic is surely necessary if a con-structive politics is to emerge, if only to avoid the absurdity of state surveillance of the length of beards or the bits of cloth people wear on their head.

Notes

1. This is an amended version of an article that first appeared in *Ethnic and Racial Studies*, 30, 4 (July 2007).
2. See C. Nordmann (ed.), *Le Foulard islamique en questions* (Paris: Editions Amsterdam, 2004), and F. Lorcerie (ed.), *La Politisation du voile: l'affaire en France, en Europe et dans le monde arabe* (Paris: L'Harmattan, 2005). Of the voluminous works on the wider questions of the French Republic, *laïcité* and Islam, see M. Gauchet, *La Religion dans la démocratie: parcours de la laïcité* (Paris: Gallimard, 1998); J. Cesari, *Musulmans et républicains: les jeunes, l'islam et la France* (Paris: Editions Complexe, 1998); J.-H. Kaltenbach and M. Tribalat, *La République et l'Islam: entre crainte et aveuglement* (Paris: Gallimard, 2002); O. Roy, *La Laïcité face à l'islam* (Paris: Editions Stock, 2005).
3. D. Macey, 'The Hijab and the Republic: Headscarves in France', *Radical Philosophy*, 125 (May–June 2004), pp. 2–6, p. 6.
4. Reported in *The Guardian*, 14 June 2006.
5. S. Trigano, *La République et les Juifs* (Paris: Gallimard, 1982).
6. S. Trigano, 'From Individual to Collectivity: the Rebirth of the "Jewish Nation" in France', in F. Malino and B. Wasserstein (eds), *The Jews in Modern France* (Hanover, NH and London: University Press of New England, 1985), p. 253.
7. G. Wilder, *The French Imperial Nation-State: Negritude and Colonial Humanism between the Two World Wars* (Chicago and London: The University of Chicago Press, 2005), p. 18.
8. E.J. Bellamy, *Affective Genealogies: Psychoanalysis, Postmodernism, and the 'Jewish Question' after Auschwitz* (Lincoln and London: University of Nebraska Press, 1997).
9. Z. Bauman, *Modernity and Ambivalence* (Cambridge: Polity, 1991).

10. J.-P. Sartre, *Anti-Semite and Jew* (New York: Schocken Books, 1948; trans. from the French *Réflexions sur la question juive*, Paris: Gallimard, 1954; first published 1946).
11. H. Arendt, *The Origins of Totalitarianism* (London: George Allen and Unwin, 1962; first published 1951).
12. J.-P. Sartre, 'Preface' to F. Fanon, *The Wretched of the Earth* (New York: Grove Press, 1966, pp. 7–26; trans. from the French *Les Damnés de la terre*, Paris, Maspero, 1961), p. 22.
13. D. Fuss, 'Interior Colonies: Frantz Fanon and the Politics of Identification', in N. C. Gibson (ed.), *Rethinking Fanon: the Continuing Dialogue* (New York: Humanity Books, 1999), p. 295.
14. Arendt, *The Origins of Totalitarianism*, p. 273.
15. Ibid., pp. 290–302.
16. In France, see especially A. Finkielkraut, *La Défaite de la pensée* (Paris: Gallimard, 1987).
17. M. Silverman, *Deconstructing the Nation: Immigration, Racism and Citizenship in Modern France* (London and New York: Routledge, 1992), pp. 19–27.
18. See especially his contributions in E. Balibar and I. Wallerstein, *Race, nation, classe: les identités ambigues* (Paris: La Découverte, 1988).
19. J.-L. Amselle, *Vers un multiculturalisme français: L'Empire de la coutume* (Paris: Flammarion, 2001; first published 1996), pp. 13–14.
20. S. Peabody and T. Stovall, 'Introduction: Race, France, Histories', in S. Peabody and T. Stovall (eds), *The Color of Liberty: Histories of Race in France* (Durham and London: Duke University Press, 2003), p. 5.
21. Macey, 'The Hijab and the Republic', p. 21.
22. N. Bancel, P. Blanchard and F. Vergès, *La République coloniale* (Paris: Hachette, 2005), p. 95.
23. Ibid., p. 98.
24. P. Weil, *Qu'est-ce qu'un Français? Histoire de la nationalité française depuis la Révolution* (Paris: Grasset, 2002), p. 275.
25. Wilder, *The French Imperial Nation-State*, p. 143. Wilder is particularly critical of Alice Conklin's approach to French Third Republic colonialism in her book *A Mission to Civilize* (Stanford: Stanford University Press, 1997) 'because Conklin conflates republicanism with universalism, which is assumed to be inherently opposed to colonial racism (reduced to particularism). She does not recognize the ways in which contradictions between universality and particularity were internal to republican, colonial, and racial discourses and practices.' Ibid., p. 7.
26. T. Shepard, *The Invention of Decolonization: the Algerian War and the Remaking of France* (Ithaca and London: Cornell University Press, 2006), pp. 7–8.
27. C. Nordmann and J. Vidal, 'La République à l'épreuve des discriminations', in Nordmann, *Le Foulard islamique en questions*, p. 11.
28. P. Gilroy, *Against Race: Imagining Political Culture beyond the Color Line* (Cambridge, Mass.: Harvard University Press, 2000), p. 42.
29. F. Fanon, *Toward the African Revolution* (Harmondsworth: Penguin Books, 1970; trans. from the French *Pour la Révolution africaine*, Paris: François Maspero, 1964).
30. Z. Bauman, *Wasted Lives: Modernity and its Outcasts* (Cambridge: Polity, 2004), p. 31; emphasis in original.

31. Finkielkraut, *La Défaite de la pensée*.
32. F. Gaspard and F. Khosrokhavar, *Le Foulard et la République* (Paris: La Découverte, 1995), p. 211.
33. This is a most sensitive debate in France. French analyses of the 'problems of the suburbs' have classically tended to highlight differences of class rather than race and dismissed the comparison between French suburbs and American-style ghettos as being the misguided analysis of race-obsessed 'Anglo-Saxon' social theorists. Loic Wacquant, for example, categorically refutes the comparison between the French 'red belt' and the American 'black belt' in cities (see for example L. Wacquant, *Parias urbains: ghetto, banlieues, Etat*, Paris: La Découverte, 2006. See also the article 'Les nouveaux parias de la république' by Stéphane Béaud and Gérard Noiriel, *Le Monde*, 20 February 2004). The tendency to downplay race as a factor in social segregation could be seen as another example of the denial of race in the republican sphere. (For a corrective to this argument and a historical account of the complex interplay between race and class in the suburbs of Paris, see T. Stovall, 'From Red Belt to Black Belt: Race, Class and Urban Marginality in Twentieth-century Paris', in Sue Peabody and Tyler Stovall (eds), *The Color of Liberty: Histories of Race in France*, Durham and London: Duke University Press, 2003, pp. 351–69.) However, as I argue above, even the comparison itself between French and American 'ghettos' frequently achieves the same goal, as the creation of ethnic ghettos in France is explained as a post-war phenomenon which accompanies the arrival of non-European immigrants and racialises the race-free republican model of assimilation hitherto in place.
34. M. Maffesoli, *Le Temps des tribus: le déclin de l'individualisme dans les sociétés de masses* (Paris: Meridiens Klincksieck, 1988).
35. S. Bouamama, 'Ethnicisation et construction idéologique d'un bouc émissaire', in Nordmann, *Le Foulard islamique en questions*, p. 42.
36. M. Silverman, *Facing Postmodernity: Contemporary French Thought on Culture and Society* (London and New York: Routledge, 1999).
37. Bauman, *Wasted Lives*, p. 66.
38. B. Stora, *La Gangrène et l'oubli: la mémoire de la guerre d'Algérie* (Paris: La Découverte, 1991).
39. Henri Giordan cited in H. Lebovics, *Bringing the Empire Back Home: France in the Global Age* (Durham and London: Duke University Press, 2004), p. 125.
40. Bancel et al., *La République coloniale*, p. ii.
41. A. Touraine, 'Égalité et différence', in M. Wieviorka and J. Ohana (eds), *La Différence culturelle: une reformulation des débats* (Paris: Balland, 2001), pp. 89–90. It should, however, be noted that, during the more recent debate on the headscarf, Touraine was opposed to extending democratic rights in breach of the law on secularism in schools, believing that the law had helped to stem the rising tide of fundamentalism. For a more complete outline of his position, see A. Renaut and A. Touraine, *Un Débat sur la laïcité* (Paris: Editions Stock, 2005).
42. See for example the debate in the late 1980s (but which persists today) on republicanism versus democracy, expressed (among others) by Régis Debray (see 'Êtes-vous républicain ou démocrate?', *Le Nouvel Observateur*, 30 November–6 December, 1989, pp. 115–21) and Alain Finkielkraut (see *La*

Défaite de la pensée, Paris: Gallimard, 1987). For a slightly more nuanced perspective by Debray on the more recent discussion of headscarves and secularism, see his contribution to the debate, as a member of the government commission set up to look into the question under the presidency of Bernard Stasi (in *Ce que nous voile le voile: La République et le sacré*, Paris: Gallimard, 2004). The commission's findings were published as *Laïcité et République* (Paris: La Documentation française, 2004).

43. In his many analyses of race and racism, Pierre-André Taguieff habitually presents universalism and particularism, assimilation and difference as the 'two logics' of racism rather than seeing more complex interconnections between them. The psychoanalyst Daniel Sibony, on the other hand, suggests that the two logics are in fact one in that both are concerned with 'fixing' the other (*Le 'Racisme' ou la haine identitaire*, Paris: Christian Bourgois, 1997, p. 36).

44. *The Guardian*, 15 November 2004.

45. F. Dubet, 'Les "différences" à l'école: entre l'égalité et la performance', in Wieviorka and Ohana, *La Différence culturelle*, p. 103.

46. P.A. Silverstein, *Algeria in France: Transpolitics, Race and Nation* (Bloomington and Indianapolis: Indiana University Press, 2004).

Select bibliography

Amselle, J.-L., *Vers un multiculturalisme français: L'Empire de la coutume* (Paris: Flammarion, 2001; first published 1996).

Arendt, H., *The Origins of Totalitarianism* (London: George Allen and Unwin, 1962; first published 1951).

Balibar, E. and Wallerstein, I., *Race, nation, classe: les identités ambigues* (Paris: La Découverte, 1988).

Bancel, N., Blanchard, P. and Vergès, F., *La République coloniale* (Paris: Hachette, 2005; first published 2003).

Bauman, Z., *Modernity and Ambivalence* (Cambridge: Polity, 1991).

Bauman, Z., *Wasted Lives: Modernity and its Outcasts* (Cambridge: Polity, 2004).

Bellamy, E. J., *Affective Genealogies: Psychoanalysis, Postmodernism, and the 'Jewish Question' after Auschwitz* (Lincoln and London: University of Nebraska Press, 1997).

Cesari, J., *Musulmans et républicains: les jeunes, l'islam et la France* (Paris: Editions Complexe, 1998).

Conklin, A., *A Mission to Civilize: the Republican Idea of Empire in France and West Africa, 1895–1930* (Stanford: Stanford University Press, 1997).

Cooper, F. and Stoler, L. (eds), *Tensions of Empire: Colonial Cultures in a Bourgeois World* (Berkeley: University of California Press, 1997).

Debray, R., *Ce que nous voile le voile: La République et le sacré* (Paris: Gallimard, 2004).

Fanon, F., *Toward the African Revolution* (Harmondsworth: Penguin Books, 1970; trans. from the French *Pour la Révolution africaine*, Paris: François Maspero, 1964).

Fanon, F., *Black Skin, White Masks* (London: Pluto Press, 1986; trans. from the French *Peau noire, masques blancs*, Paris: Seuil, 1952).

74   *The Construction of Minority Identities in France and Britain*

Finkielkraut, A., *La Défaite de la pensée* (Paris: Gallimard, 1987).
Galster, I. (ed.), *Sartre et les juifs* (Paris: La Découverte, 2005).
Gaspard, F. and Khosrokhavar, F., *Le Foulard et la République* (Paris: La Découverte, 1995).
Gauchet, M., *La Religion dans la démocratie: parcours de la laïcité* (Paris: Gallimard, 1998).
Gibson, N.C. (ed.), *Rethinking Fanon: the Continuing Dialogue* (New York: Humanity Books, 1999), pp. 294–328.
Gilroy, P., *Against Race: Imagining Political Culture beyond the Color Line* (Cambridge, Mass.: Harvard University Press, 2000).
House, J. and MacMaster, N., *Paris 1961: Algerians, State Terror and Memory* (Oxford: Oxford University Press, 2006).
Kaltenbach, J.-H. and Tribalat, M., *La République et l'Islam: entre crainte et aveuglement* (Paris: Gallimard, 2002).
Lebovics, H., *Bringing the Empire Back Home: France in the Global Age* (Durham and London: Duke University Press, 2004).
Lorcerie, F. (ed.), *La Politisation du voile: l'affaire en France, en Europe et dans le monde arabe* (Paris: L'Harmattan, 2005).
Macey, D., *Frantz Fanon: a Life* (London: Granta Books, 2000).
Maffesoli, M., *Le Temps des tribus: le déclin de l'individualisme dans les sociétés de masses* (Paris: Meridiens Klincksieck, 1988).
Malino, F. and Wasserstein, B. (eds) *The Jews in Modern France* (Hanover, NH and London: University Press of New England, 1985).
Noiriel, G., *Le Creuset français: Histoire de l'immigration X1Xe–XXe siècles* (Paris: Seuil, 1988).
Nordmann, C. (ed.) *Le Foulard islamique en questions* (Paris: Editions Amsterdam, 2004).
Peabody, S. and Stovall, T. (eds), *The Color of Liberty: Histories of Race in France* (Durham and London: Duke University Press, 2003).
Renaut, A. and Touraine, A., *Un Débat sur la laïcité* (Paris: Editions Stock, 2005).
Roy, O., *La Laïcité face à l'islam* (Paris: Editions Stock, 2005).
Sartre, J.-P., *Anti-Semite and Jew* (New York: Schocken Books, 1948; trans. from the French *Réflexions sur la question juive*, Paris: Gallimard, 1954; first published 1946).
Shepard, T., *The Invention of Decolonization: the Algerian War and the Remaking of France* (Ithaca and London: Cornell University Press, 2006).
Sibony, D., *Le 'Racisme' ou la haine identitaire* (Paris: Christian Bourgois, 1997).
Silverman, M., *Deconstructing the Nation: Immigration, Racism and Citizenship in Modern France* (London and New York: Routledge, 1992).
Silverman, M., *Facing Postmodernity: Contemporary French Thought on Culture and Society* (London and New York: Routledge, 1999).
Silverstein, P. A., *Algeria in France: Transpolitics, Race and Nation* (Bloomington and Indianapolis: Indiana University Press, 2004).
Stoler, A. L., *Race and the Education of Desire: Foucault's History of Sexuality and the Colonial Order of Things* (Durham and London: Duke University Press, 1995).
Stora, B., *La Gangrène et l'oubli: la mémoire de la guerre d'Algérie* (Paris: La Découverte, 1991).
Tagueiff P.-A. *Les Fins de l'anti-racisme* (Paris: Editions Michalon, 1995).
Trigano, S., *La République et les Juifs* (Paris: Gallimard, 1982).

Wacquant, L., *Parias urbains: ghetto, banlieues, Etat* (Paris: La Découverte, 2006).

Weil, P., *Qu'est-ce qu'un Français? Histoire de la nationalité française depuis la Révolution* (Paris: Grasset, 2002).

Wieviorka, M. and Ohana, J. (eds), *La Différence culturelle: une reformulation des débats* (Paris: Balland, 2001).

Wilder, G., *The French Imperial Nation-State: Negritude and Colonial Humanism between the Two World Wars* (Chicago and London: The University of Chicago Press, 2005).

Part II

Experiencing the Construction of Minority Identities

5
Shifting Sociocultural Identities: Young People of North African Origin in France

Nadia Kiwan

Introduction

This chapter will ask to what extent the idea of the construction of a minority identity is pertinent or appropriate to the *problématique* of young people of North African origin living in stigmatised urban settings in contemporary France. Is there a conscious or collective articulation of a culturally and socially specific experience linking this 'post-migrant' generation together? In the last 25 years, many social and political commentators, in both the academic and media worlds, have focused much attention on the descendants of North African immigrants to France. Some have based their analyses on questions of cultural difference and its implications in an 'indivisible' republican body politic. Others have paid more attention to more social questions such as education, employment and urban life. Both types of approach have been premised on the notion of integration. However, there has been relatively little work which has simultaneously incorporated a cultural and social approach to the discussions of the life trajectories and experiences of the young post-migrants of North African descent in France. The empirical research on which this chapter is based arises out of an attempt to rearticulate social and cultural perspectives with regard to this population. In this chapter we will look at how collective experience among young people of North African origin is constantly sliding between cultural and social poles of identification. The 'cultural' refers to how one might define oneself in relation to one's national/regional, linguistic or 'ethnic' origins.[1] The 'social' can be understood as how actors define themselves in relation to their social origins, i.e. in terms of economic status, spatial identity (where they live, such as a *cité HLM*/social housing estate or *pavillon*/detached house for example) or 'class' background.

The first part of the chapter will concentrate on a brief overview of the recent intellectual and public debates concerning young people of North African origin in France. The second part will focus on the contrast between the experiences of the young people concerned and those debates. This part will draw on empirical work and illustrate how the young people in question are continuously circulating between social and cultural forms of identification. It will also show how they simultaneously draw on community-oriented and more universal elements of identity. Finally, the third part of this chapter will show how, although the young people mobilised a highly reflexive sense of sociocultural identity, this articulation of the social and cultural often retains an individual rather than collective dimension. The chapter will conclude with some discussion of *why* it then becomes difficult to describe this sample of young people of North African origin as forming a collective 'minority' actor in the public sphere. More importantly, the wider implications regarding the possible emergence of a 'minority' French-North African collective actor will be considered.

The parameters of the debate

Much of the recent French intellectual and political debate surrounding immigration has tended either to focus on the social *or* cultural implications of the emergence of the so-called 'second' and 'third' generations. For example, a significant amount of the intellectual and public discussions over the last 30 years has tended to focus on more socio-economic questions such as tensions in France's less well-off urban peripheries and issues relating to social integration. Other debates have tended to focus purely on more cultural questions, such as how and if the French Republic should deal with the 'challenge' posed by 'cultural difference'. One of the main limitations in these discussions has been that debates have either tended to inflate the socio-economic *or* the cultural and have, as a result, failed to fully address both the social and cultural dimensions of immigration and post-migrant populations.

The 'challenge' of cultural difference

The last 20–30 years in France have seen the development of a debate which has focused on the question of cultural difference and the challenge this poses to the republican understanding of the public sphere as culturally 'neutral'. The 1980s and 1990s in particular were characterised by a certain sense of malaise due to a number of major economic and social transformations: deindustrialisation, institutional change in the education, justice and public service systems. The permanent settlement of 'non-European origin' immigrants also led to a heightened sensitivity to visible and perceived 'cultural' difference. All these factors led to the emergence of a debate surrounding how the Republic should deal with the 'cultural difference' of its immigrant and post-migrant populations. As Michel Wieviorka has pointed out, the debate about cultural difference and increasing demands for official recognition of difference by 'minority' groups was generally divided into two 'camps', the *républicains* and the *démocrates*. The *républicains* argued that any recognition of cultural difference in the public sphere would be contrary to the principles of the 'one and indivisible' Republic and would therefore have a devastating effect. Examples such as civil-war Lebanon or the war in ex-Yugoslavia were often cited as the road France could be going down, if it embraced multiculturalism.[2] The opposing camp, the *démocrates*, who were less anxious about the recognition of difference, were accused by the *républicains* of being *communautaristes* (roughly translatable as communitarians) and of wanting to undermine republican values. One of the main images throughout this debate was the United States, or more specifically, 'American multiculturalism', which was caricatured by the *républicaniste* camp, who argued that the recognition of cultural difference would lead to the increasing 'ghettoisation' of French society.

The over-focus on the socio-economic

In contrast to the discussions which centred on the notion of cultural difference, there has been a lot of work carried out on issues relating to the *banlieue* (town peripheries), urban violence, urban insecurity, etc. These discussions, both academic and public, have foregrounded more socio-economic analyses, to the extent that discussions of culture have not been fully integrated. For example, in the intellectual debate, Francois Dubet's book *La Galère* can be seen as one of the early pieces of research, which in some sense set the tone for later work around youth in stigmatised *banlieue* settings.[3] What is striking in Dubet's book and other research around themes of the *banlieue* as developed by David Lepoutre, Henri Rey and others is the almost over-focus on the social. For example, although a large proportion of the individuals who took part in his study were of North African origin, Dubet claims that their experiences of exclusion (although somewhat heightened among those of North African origin) are not fundamentally different from their 'French origin' counterparts. Yet, they are still referred to as 'jeunes immigrés' ('young immigrants'), thus distinguishing them from their 'French' ('français de souche') peers.[4] Furthermore, although Lepoutre's study of middle-school pupils in La Courneuve foregrounds the notion of a 'système culturel', his understanding of a cultural system is above all social, as he describes the everyday world of his informants in terms of a 'culture des rues'.[5]

It is therefore possible to formulate a critique of the literature on immigration (and its related issues) based on two observations. On the one hand, a lot of intellectual discourses have remained influenced by the ideological oppositions between universalism and particularism, where the individual citizen is opposed to the community. Here it would seem that almost too much weight is given to culturalist paradigms. On the other hand, intellectual discourses relating to the *banlieue* often pay so much attention to socio-economic factors, to the extent that the fact that many of the *banlieues* which occupy the social *imaginaire* (imagination) and reality are also inhabited by large populations of immigrant origin, is largely ignored.

So what about the discourses generated by those 'on the ground'? How might they relate to the public and intellectual discourses which privilege normative debates about integration, universalism and particularism and which tend to adopt either overly cultural/asocial or overly social/acultural enquiries into immigrant-origin youth?

In an attempt to reconstitute a social *and* cultural approach to the *problématique* of immigrant and post-migrant populations in France, this chapter has been based on the findings of an empirical study in Aubervilliers, a town in the north-east periphery of Paris. Over the course of 12 months, 64 young people of North African background, aged between 16 and 31, were interviewed, the main objective being to look more closely at cultural and social modes of identification. In addition, a significant element of the fieldwork examined the relationship between this age group and civil society associations, since the involvement in associations could be seen as representing an 'external' form of self-realisation in the public space.[6] The qualitative approach adopted was designed to offset the numerical limitations of the sample, and while clearly such a study remains focused and limited in geographical terms, certain empirical and theoretical generalisations can be made about it, as shall be shown below.

Aubervilliers is a town which lies on the north-east outskirts of Paris. It has a long history as a worker and migrant town. The town's immigrants first came from Italy, Spain, Portugal, then the Maghreb and lastly, sub-Saharan Africa and the Indian subcontinent. The last census recorded 29.7 per cent of the 63,524 inhabitants as being of foreign nationality and three-quarters of these nationals are from outside the European Union. This is the second-highest proportion of foreign nationals in the *département*, the highest proportion being 33 per cent. This means that many more inhabitants are, as a result, of 'foreign *origin*' as well, since those born in France can obtain French nationality at the age of 18. A large proportion (41.3 per cent) of its population lives in social housing and the unemployment rate is high – 22.6 per cent compared to an average of 11.5 per cent for the Ile-de-France region. In addition, a high proportion of young people residing in the town (aged between 16 and 25) are underqualified (33.3 per cent of the population have no qualifications); 41 per cent of the town's active population are described as 'workers'.[7]

Lived experiences in Aubervilliers

How do the various discourses relating to immigrant and post-migrant populations in France relate to the lived experiences of, and modes of identification prevalent among, these individuals? More importantly, does the notion of a 'minority identity' correspond to their *problématique*? Certainly, it would be inaccurate to describe the young people who were interviewed as engaging with a minority identity which is expressed in purely *ethnic* or cultural terms. Rather, through interviewing and participant observation it became clear that the young people in question are continuously circulating between social and cultural forms of identification, while simultaneously drawing on community-oriented and more universal elements of identity.

The cultural

Many of the young people who were interviewed adopted rather ethnicised modes of self-presentation in some contexts. However, at other points in the interviews or in different contexts, they engaged much more with socio-economic perspectives on their own lives. For example, Aicha, a 28-year-old care auxiliary trainee, who was born in Algeria and came to France at the age of two (and who is an Algerian national), makes a point of presenting herself as '*une Kabyle*'.[8] Most of her close friends are *kabyle* and she admits that she has difficulty establishing close friendships with young people of Algerian *Arab* origin.[9] Other interviewees, high-school pupils and university student, Khadija, Naima and Waleed, also underline the fact that they are Moroccan Berbers as opposed to Moroccan Arabs. As Waleed comments: *'Je suis Shleh, faut pas confondre!'*[10] However, such ethnicised modes of identification are not always self-assigned either. For example, Mahmoud, a 19-year-old high-school pupil who was born in Paris and holds French–Algerian dual nationality, claims that he sees himself as an Arab because that is how others perceive him:

> Je me vois par rapport à comment on me juge, comme un Arabe. On me jugerait comme un Français, je me verrais comme un Français. Je me vois par rapport à comment on me juge, je sais que je suis un Arabe. Les gens me voient comme un Arabe, je suis arabe, je suis fier de l'être.[11]

In relation to the issue of the parents' country of origin, many of the interviewees adopted a position which seemed to be premised on cultural difference and distinctiveness. For example, a number of notably male interviewees, all of whom were born in France, argue that they would like to retire to their parents' country of origin. They therefore seem to reproduce their parents' discourses and trajectories to a certain extent. Mahmoud, for example, presents himself as a first–generation immigrant and evokes his plans to build a house in Algeria so that he can live there later in life: '... c'est le rêve des immigrés ça ... de repartir, faire construire une maison, une fois qu'ils vieillissent, ils veulent retourner dans leurs pays, c'est ce que tout le monde fait, c'est ce que nous ferons aussi ...'.[12] Fouad (a 31-year-old unemployed volunteer in a local association, born in France and with French–Algerian nationality) also talks about his desire to 'return' to Algeria, where he would like to establish his own business. He dreams of leaving France and setting up a music production company:

> Je vois vraiment pas mon avenir ici. Je vois plus mon avenir là-bas [...] je me vois pas faire de très grandes choses en France ... je me vois plus là-bas, et vivre là-bas [...] j'ai connu personnellement l'Algérie en quatre-vingt treize, pour des enterrements et personnellement, je suis tombé complètement amoureux de ce pays [...] Moi, personnellement, l'identité elle est vraiment ancrée [là-bas].[13]

This process of idealising the parents' country of origin, in Fouad's case, contrasts with his critique of post-migrant cultural and religious practice in Aubervilliers. He is especially critical of the way in which many of the post-migrant youth of North African origin in Aubervilliers observe the fasting month of Ramadan: '... les trois quarts ici, c'est une question plus d'identité que de religion [...] ici, c'est le suivi, l'endoctrinement [...] oui, suivre le troupeau'. (... three-quarters of them here, it's more a question of identity than religion [...] here, it's copying the rest of them, indoctrination [...], yes, following the herd'.)[14] It is significant that Fouad mentions Ramadan, since this is a period which takes on a certain social significance in Aubervilliers. Indeed, Georg Simmel's observations about the significance and effects of religious festivals on the sense of group unity does seem to hold true in Aubervilliers. In particular Simmel observed that '... religious festivals [...] display in the clearest possible form the unity of all those captured by the same religious excitement...'[15] It seems that this notion of excitement that Simmel wrote about is highly relevant to some of the interviewees' discourse on Ramadan. Fawzia, a 17-year-old high-school pupil, who was born in France to Algerian parents, argues that Ramadan means that pupils from all backgrounds mix and share the 'fasting experience' whether they are Muslim or not. Youth worker 'Sara' also echoes this claim: 'Il y a un phénomène bizarre pendant le jeûne. Tout le monde jeûne, même les Français jeûnent.' ('There's a strange phenomenon here during the fast. Everyone fasts, even the French fast.')[16]

Other 'sites' for ethnicised or cultural modes of identification concern language and, rather unsurprisingly perhaps, marriage. With regard to language, there are two types of attitude which dominate: 'group unity' and 'heritage'. Interviewees often used their knowledge of Arabic or Tamazight ('Berber') in order to try to demonstrate and valorise their cultural knowledge in front of non-Arabic or Tamazight speakers. Alternatively, they use their knowledge in a spirit of competition where individuals often want to prove that they are just as much part of what Benedict Anderson would call the 'imagined' linguistic community, as their peers.[17]

In much of the social sciences literature about migrant groups or 'minorities', marriage practices are often cited as one of most significant ways of measuring the extent to which migrant families and their children have become 'integrated' or even 'assimilated' into the mainstream society or to what extent they have maintained traditional (in the sense of family-oriented) values. However, as Nacira Guénif points out in her study of young women of North African origin and their families, the very act of migration for the first generation of immigrants, constitutes in itself a break with the past and with 'traditional' practices in the country of origin.[18] So marriage should not simply be conceptualised as an area of the interviewees' lives which is *either* governed by 'traditional' family values *or* the individual's preferences. Most of the interviewees who were questioned about marriage demonstrated a rather subjective stance towards their choice of future marriage partner where they took into account parental wishes and expectations as well as their own. However, many expressed conflicting ideas, at first claiming that they would marry the partner of their choice, regardless of their parents, and then retreating on this initial stance later on in the interview. Once again there seem to exist two dominant models with regards to marriage: 'mentality' and group unity or peer pressure. A significant number of interviewees (9 out of the 26 who were asked about future marriage partners), discuss marriage partners in terms of community and 'heritage'. The notion of having the same 'mentality' or outlook, where cultural 'origins' are the 'assessment criteria', was quite prevalent among the male and female interviewees.

The social

Of course, one should be aware that by asking individuals about their cultural origins, use of language and self-perception, that one runs the risk of 'producing' ethnicised modes of identification in their responses. Nevertheless, even the interviews with individuals and groups revealed modes of identification which were continually shifting from more cultural to social or socio-economic emphasis. For example, the *banlieue* (suburb) which, generally, has come to signify the less well-off urban peripheries of Paris and other major French cities, plays an extremely important role in the construction of identities among the young men and women. Although *la banlieue* has in the public *imaginaire* been consistently ethnicised, both implicitly and explicitly, the interviewees did not necessarily conceive of Aubervilliers and *la banlieue* to the north of Paris in 'ethnic' terms. However, this does not mean that the *banlieue* is not of key collective significance. For example, the notion of solidarity is often cited by interviewees as being a unique feature of living in the *banlieue*. Yet they reject the idea that there may be more solidarity between people in the urban peripheries because many of the inhabitants are of North African or sub-Saharan African origin. Mona, a French-born 17-year-old high-school pupil whose parents are Algerian, argues that in Aubervilliers there is more solidarity than in Paris: 'Ici on est plus solidaire que là-bas je trouve. [...] On est pas forcément solidaire parce qu'on est tous maghrébin, je sais pas pourquoi.' ('Here there's more solidarity than there, I think. [...] We're not necessarily more united because we're all Maghrebi, I don't know why.)'[19]

Another pupil, Fawzia echoes this stance: 'Aubervilliers, tout le monde se connaît, c'est des choses comme ça. Je pense pas que c'est les origines....' ('Everybody knows each other in Aubervilliers, it's things like that. I don't think that it's a question of origins...').[20]

In addition to a relatively pronounced sense of identity with regards to the *banlieue*, which is conceived of as a socio-economic and cultural 'imagined community' (to borrow Benedict Anderson's terminology once more), existing in opposition to Paris, some interviewees also reveal the fact they enjoy close ties with their immediate *quartier* (neighbourhood).[21] These ties are expressed in a number of ways. For example, some 29 interviewees (about half of the sample) are, or have been, involved as youth workers in local neighbourhood associations that organise sociocultural, educational and sporting activities for young people in a particular *quartier* or housing estate (*cité*).

There is quite a widespread acceptance and praise of young people who are seen to be involved with their immediate community in the *cité* or neighbourhood where they live. The theme of the idealised image of the *grand frère* (older brother) who protects their younger brothers and sisters (or their younger female and male acquaintances) from the same housing estate or neighbourhood is very prevalent in the respondents' experiences. It develops possibly as a result of the relative 'absence' of the parents who make up the first generation of immigrants (the father is a largely invisible figure in the interviewees' presentation of their experiences, often either because he works long hours or is 'eclipsed' at home due to long-term unemployment or, in quite a few cases, ill health). Some mothers and fathers are absent or in the background because of their lack of fluency in French. So it is the eldest brothers and sisters who become the parents since it is they who deal with many of the administrative and practical family matters such as banking, health care, etc. Older brothers and sisters may also have a significant influence on the educational and career paths of their younger brothers and sisters since the parents are often unable to advise their children. The role of the *grand frère* is of course played by some biological brothers and sisters but it can also take on a more social meaning in the sense that the older inhabitants of the *cité* or the *quartier* are expected to look after the younger residents. Hence the *animateur* can be seen as the institutionalisation of the *grand frère* model as well as part of a process of erosion of paternal authority and capability once migration has taken place. The *grand frère* phenomenon is thus possibly linked with the high number of young people in the sample who were or had at one point been an *animateur* or *animatrice* in a youth association.

However, the importance of the *quartier* or neighbourhood reference is not generally ethnicised, even among those men and women who appear to adopt rather a communitarian stance in relation to other issues. Rather it is one based on social experience and social origins.

Furthermore, while some interviewees construct a sense of self-perception which is very much based on a notion of cultural embeddedness, in relation to political life, they generally are not willing to buy into the notion of 'ethnic minority' status. Here, the young men and women either do not even seem to regard the possibility of specific ethnic minority demands as an option or when they do, they tend to reject it. For example, Touran, a 21-year-old university student of Algerian origin, who at other times engages with themes of cultural embeddedness and 'difference', argues that when it comes to politics, cultural origins should not be made into an issue. When asked on what basis he would make political claims he replies: 'Moi en tant tout simplement que jeune parce que des jeunes ici, il y a des Français dans mon quartier qui triment autant que moi [...] c'est clair donc non en tant que jeune, ni d'origine maghrébine, ni de musulman [...] en tant que jeune ... '.[22] Similarly, although Abdel Majid adopts a more 'community' oriented approach to religion and marriage, he argues that it is preferable to make social and political claims 'en tant que jeune tout simplement'.[23] Many of the political demands that the young people tend to make are linked to access to greater employment opportunities. However they do not openly recognise that there may be a difference of experience between those youths of North African origin and those who are not, despite both young men and women's repeated references to their experience or fear of racial discrimination. It would thus seem that these interviewees have interiorised certain republican and universalist norms, namely that political or social demands should be made by the 'culturally unattached' citizen, rather than by a citizen who draws attention to his/her difference. This calls to mind the accuracy of sociologist Didier Lapeyronnie's comment that: 'L'immigré cherche à obtenir la reconnaissance d'une identité qu'il souhaite invisible.'[24] ('The immigrant looks to obtain recognition of an identity which he wishes to remain invisible.') The paradoxical shifting from 'community' stances regarding marriage, self-presentation or Islam, to more universalist or colour-blind strategies regarding political or social claims reveals an unwillingness to carry a 'minority identity' over into the public sphere.

More significantly, it would seem then that the young people in question are unfamiliar with the notion of making formal social or political demands. 'Sara', a 26-year-old *animatrice* of Moroccan origin who works with a significant proportion of the younger interviewees at a local youth centre, comments that there is generally no sense of political claims among the young people she works with.[25] Likewise, 'Djamel', a 31-year-old *conseiller principal d'éducation* (chief school supervisor) of Algerian origin, remarks on the differences between his, more politically aware generation and the current 16–25 age bracket. Certainly, Djamel's observations point to the fact that the reference to a working-class identity, which, historically, structured the political and social life of the *banlieues rouges* (the traditionally communist-dominated outer suburbs) the interviewees' fathers knew, has, by and large, disappeared.

A fluid subjectivity

Many of the young people who took part in the field study were able to demonstrate a subjective sense of sociocultural identity. This subjectivity stems out of a capacity to simultaneously draw on community-oriented and more universal elements of identity, thus rejecting familiar universalism–particularism dichotomies. At times, the young men and women's cultural 'background' becomes a motor for this subjective agency. For example, subjectivity is relevant when 'Leila', a high-school pupil who was born in France but whose parents are Algerian, argues that she has every intention of becoming a primary-school teacher in the French public sector, despite the fact that she wears a headscarf and may subsequently face certain obstacles.[26] However, although the young people mobilised a subjective sense of sociocultural identity, this articulation of the social and cultural often retains an individual rather than collective dimension. In other words, it is not accurate to describe young people of North African origin as forming a collective 'minority' actor in the public sphere. As shown in the previous section, despite the articulation of nuanced social and cultural identities on an individual level, the interviewees did not tend to see the need for the construction of a public or politicised minority identity which would be simultaneously based on a social and cultural/'ethnic' understanding of minority. This was evident when interviewees discussed their relationship to the political process (see above) but also towards associational life.

Associational life

An important element of the field study carried out in Aubervilliers encompassed the issue of civil society associations and young post-migrants' participation in associations of all kinds – cultural, socio-educational, religious, neighbourhood and sporting. Quite a network of civil society associations has grown up in France's urban peripheries, especially among migrant and post-migrant populations. The initial explosion of immigrant associations dates back to 1981 when the Mitterrand government made it legal for foreign nationals to set up their own associations. While undertaking the empirical research in Aubervilliers, it became increasingly clear that a relatively high proportion of the interviewees were involved in local civil society associations and their activities. Did such a noticeable level of involvement reflect a renewed conflictualisation of sociocultural concerns or a platform for the public construction of a simultaneously social and cultural 'minority identity'?

Before discussing the nature of youth involvement in associations, it is useful to contextualise further the relevance of civil society associations in a town like Aubervilliers. In her extensive study of the development of associations, political scientist Martine Barthélémy argues that what we call associations in France today, have been intrinsically linked with the workers' movement, syndicalism and the transformations in political organisation which accompanied the development of socialist ideas. Barthélemy also shows that the recognition of the notion of a 'social' citizenship as opposed to the more classic 'political' citizenship which historically excluded many groups such as women and still excludes non-EU nationals, can be seen as the background to the legal recognition of the right of individuals to associate. In July 1901, the right to form an association in France was legalised. Barthélemy cites Jean-Paul Martin who argues that from the outset, 'good' associations were seen to be those that would become '[des] écoles[s] de la démocratie' (schools of democracy) and work *in tandem* with the state in the general interest.[27] However, views have differed on the role of associations, some observers regarding them as civil society's necessary *counterbalance* to the state and government.

So it is possible to consider associations in France as providing an alternative site for political engagement, despite occupying that awkward position, observed by Adil Jazouli, of wanting to remain *outside* of the political process, and at the same time searching for recognition and integration *into* the political process.[28] Involvement in associations among young people of immigrant origin may not necessarily be explicitly political but instead often point merely towards issues of social and cultural identification in the public space. However, it is still significant that the majority of interviewees were not involved in associations of a cultural/ethnic 'community' nature.

The young men who took part in the field research were overwhelmingly involved in associations which provide leisure activities as well as professional advice. In fact, all of the young men can be described as being linked to a leisure-oriented or educational association. Only one young man is involved in a culturally oriented association (Tamazight [Berber] lessons in an association) and only two male interviewees were involved in an association of a religious nature, that is, they both refer to their attendance of a local mosque (in France, many mosques have the status of a cultural association). It would seem then, that the main motivation for becoming involved in associations is the interviewees' fear of continuing social and economic marginalisation.

One difference between the young men and women interviewees is that young women are proportionally less involved in associations which provide leisure activities and educational support than their male counterparts. The young women respondents also tended to be more involved in associations with a cultural dimension than men. The most common reason for participating in a cultural association among the young women was to learn either Arabic or Tamazight. Once again only a tiny minority of the sample (two) frequent a religious association.

Quite a few interviewees are involved in associations on a voluntary basis, for instance during a fairly protracted period of unemployment or as a part-time employee (*vacataire*). This voluntary or paid work often entails the provision of assistance at youth clubs and therefore implies a certain degree of investment in the local community and local community issues. So it could be argued that there is a fairly significant degree of engagement with the immediate social surroundings among the interviewees. However, it must be acknowledged that many young people tend to see associations as an alternative employment market, or at least as a factor which will allow them to gain work experience and then proceed to employment with a more impressive curriculum vitae. Some interviewees explain that they became an *animateur* in their local *association de quartier* by accident but that it served them well since a part-time job affords some financial independence while they are still students. Others set up their own association so as to be able to gain some practical *animation* experience after obtaining the BAFA (youth and leisure work qualification) and that as soon as they found employment, they abandoned their voluntary activities (homework clubs, excursions, etc.). Others also claim to have 'fallen' into *animation* by accident because it was suggested to them by people in their entourage.

While this tendency to see associations as an alternative employment market should be seen in the context of the unemployment crisis affecting young and post-migrant populations, it does point to the fact that there exists little sense of a conflictualisation of relations between young post-migrants and the authorities in the public space. Conflictualisation is used here in the positive, self-affirming sense. Surely, in order for a conflictualised stance to emerge, a sense of minority or culturally/socially specific identity would have to be articulated. Yet this conscious articulation of a minority sociocultural identity on a collective level eludes the young people who took part in the field research, despite very clear, yet individually expressed claims for greater equal opportunities and an end to racial discrimination. So civil associational involvement would seem to be a pragmatic and individualised way in which these young people deal with the fear of social exclusion regarding access to employment, education and culture. In this sense then, the interviewees can be seen to be part of a generalised context of increased political apathy and as part of a wider 'apolitical' generation since associations, as representative 'units' of civil society, could potentially be sites for the collective expression of a sociocultural minority identity, because they are exterior to the increasingly challenged mainstream party political process. However, the political apathy and lack of an articulated minority identity among the interviewees could turn out to be more serious in terms of its consequences than it is for their counterparts of non-immigrant origin, whose concerns with regard to social exclusion are not related to issues of racial discrimination.

Conclusions

One has to ask if this apparent failure to mobilise a collective self-consciousness in terms of a cultural/ethnic minority identity or status will persist. One could of course argue that the riots of October–November 2005 signalled just such a *prise de conscience* (collective awakening) of many young people of North African and *banlieue* origin. Indeed, Aubervilliers was affected during this period. One hundred and four cars were burnt, 30 bins were set alight and 23 buildings were damaged by fire, two of which were severely damaged (a school gym and a local depot) and two police officers and a youth were injured by rubber bullets.[29] However, for a number of reasons, it is problematic to take the analysis of a collective *political* awakening too far. One of these reasons relates to the ephemeral nature of the events. One cannot ignore the fact that some participants in the riots were simply responding to the provocations of the Interior Minister Nicolas Sarkozy, rather than engaging in some sort of action with more medium to long-term motivations. Furthermore, the fact that the overwhelming majority of the rioters were young men and boys excludes the voice and perspectives of women from this moment of *prise de conscience*. Finally, the relatively young age of the rioters (the majority of them were aged between 14 and 20) and the non-involvement of the 20–30 age group, also limit the argument that the riots signalled the emergence of a social movement.[30]

This is not to suggest that rioters had nothing to say. Indeed, as Didier Lapeyronnie points out, the riots of October and November 2005 *did* have a social signification, contrary to what many political and academic commentators have claimed.[31] They were therefore not the irrational and senseless attempts of an enraged mob in Lapeyronnie's view. Rather, the riots can be interpreted as stemming from a rational understanding of specific social and political mechanisms which perpetuate the situation of exclusion which many of the rioters find themselves in (geographical and educational relegation, and racism). However, the absence of specific *revendications* or demands on the part of the rioters makes it difficult to understand this period as marking the emergence of a collective *politicised* consciousness on the part of young people in the *banlieues*. Furthermore, although it cannot be denied that there was a significant racialised dimension to the riots (both in terms of the media and political discourses which were adopted at the time), the rioters did not, according to Lapeyronnie, foreground any sense of common ethnicity. Nor did they reveal any common ideological motivation, according to Laurent Muchielli and Abderrahim Aït Omar.[32]

Despite the heavy-handedness of the government's response to the riots and the young people in the *banlieue* more broadly, the government's ongoing national strategy for equality of opportunity (*Stratégie nationale pour l'égalité des chances*), launched in autumn 2004, may signal a greater willingness to address the shortcomings of the Republic's egalitarian project. An optimistic reading of this development might argue that the strategy's proposal to recruit French nationals 'of foreign origin' or from the overseas territories through an *action positive* scheme (a new term which resembles the previously rejected 'American' 'affirmative action') might consequently pre-empt the *need* for post-migrants of North African origin to construct a specific minority identity based not only on social disadvantage but on a collective experience of racial, cultural and religious discrimination. However, the introduction of legislation banning the wearing of conspicuous religious symbols in public schools in the same year signals a reluctance to acknowledge the greater cultural complexity in contemporary France. This legislation, passed in March 2004 and applicable from September 2004 onwards, has had repercussions beyond the school gates, with some Muslim women claiming that they have been subjected to discriminatory practices within universities and the workplace. More broadly though, the introduction of the law as well as the sustained period of intense public debate prior to its promulgation, and this in spite of the fact that in terms of quantative significance, the numbers of religious symbols (and particularly 'Islamic' headscarves) had actually been falling since the previous *affaire du foulard* in 1994, reveals how at a deeper level, the Republic has more difficulty dealing with some forms of difference than others (in 1994–95, 3000 religious symbols had been counted; in 2003–4 the figure stood at 1465).[33]

The mobilisation of certain French Muslim groups such as Le Comité 15 mars et libertés in reaction to the religious symbols legislation in March 2004, suggests that the law which aimed to promote the universality of the public space, may in fact have backfired and fuelled the public emergence of a minority ethnicised/religious identity. Beyond such conservative and religiously motivated opposition to the law, the two years which have followed the new law have also seen the emergence of secular groups which criticise the legislation. Such is the case of the Collectif une École pour Toutes et Tous which groups together the MRAP (Mouvement contre le Racisme et pour l'Amitié entre les Peuples), trade union activists and also associations such as Femmes Plurielles or Femmes Publiques. A further example of the emergence of a secular opposition to the law can be found within the Mouvement des Indigènes de la République which denounced the legislation as 'discriminatory'.[34] The *Appel* was initiated by a range of associations that included TouTEsegaux.net, ATMF (Association des Travailleurs Maghrébins de France) and a number of individuals. It has since been signed by hundreds of people (from well-known academics to high-school pupils). However, it is not the law in itself or by itself which may signal the future emergence of a minority identity among young people of North African origin. Rather, it is its place among a series of measures and debates which continue to stigmatise this population, thus exacerbating mechanisms of social, racial and cultural discrimination, which may contribute to the future forging of a widespread sense of minority *politicised* identity, as potentially exemplified by the Mouvement des Indigenes de la République.

Notes

1. Notions of 'culture' and 'class' in the humanities and social sciences are, of course, more complex. However, it is beyond the scope of this chapter to discuss these concepts in great depth and readers should regard the 'definitions' provided in this section as merely introducing the general framework of the empirical work undertaken for this piece of research.
2. M. Wieviorka, *La Différence culturelle: une reformulation des débats* (Paris: Balland, 2001), pp. 7–14.
3. F. Dubet, *La Galère: jeunes en survie* (Paris: Fayard, 1997). *La galère* signifies boredom or great difficulty.
4. While the expression *français de souche* (French origin) is a highly problematic one, not least because it fails to capture the historically hybrid nature of the French population, it is a term used quite frequently (but mostly in 'inverted commas') to denote those individuals who have no obvious recent family history of immigration to France.
5. D. Lepoutre, *Coeur de banlieue: codes, rites et langages* (Paris: Odile Jacob, 2001), p. 418 and p. 28.
6. This figure does not include the association employees and *animateurs*, *éducateurs* (youth workers) teachers, policemen and municipally elected *députés* (councillors) who were also interviewed as part of the field research. By 'of North African background/origin' I am referring to individuals who may have been born in France to North African parents or who may have come to France from Algeria, Morocco or Tunisia as children or adolescents. All interviews were semi-structured.
7. Statistics from *Recensement de la population de 1999: les grandes tendances à Aubervilliers et des comparaisons départementales et régionales* (Observatoire de la Société Locale, Mairie d'Aubervilliers, March 2001) and A. Foussat, *Aubervilliers à la page*, No. 5 (Observatoire de la Société Locale, Mairie d'Aubervilliers, December 1999). This study by A. Foussat contains statistics taken from the earlier 1990 census.
8. Kabylia is the region in the north-east of Algeria where the non-Arab, Tamazight speakers or 'Berbers' originate from.
9. Author's interview with 'Aicha', 12/12/00, 14/12/00.
10. Author's interview with 'Waleed', February 2001.
11. Author's interview with 'Fayçal', 'Mahmoud' and 'Razak', 13/09/01. 'I see myself in relation to how people perceive me, as an Arab. If they perceived me as a French person, I'd see myself as a French person. I see myself according to how people perceive me; I know that I'm an Arab. People see me as an Arab, I'm Arab, and proud to be one.' All translations are by the author unless otherwise stated.
12. Author's interview with 'Faycal', 'Mahmoud' and 'Razak', 13/09/01. 'That's every immigrant's dream that … to go back, build a house, once they're old, they want to return to their countries, that's what everyone does, that's what we'll do as well …'.
13. Author's interview with 'Fouad' and 'Yacine', 05/07/01. 'I really don't see my future here. I see my future more over there […] I don't see myself doing much in France … I see myself more over there, living there […] I personally

got to know Algeria in '93, for a funeral and I fell completely in love with the country. [...] For me, my identity is really rooted [over there].'

14. Ibid.
15. G. Simmel, *Essays on Religion*, ed. and trans. by H. J. Helle in collaboration with L. Nieder (New Haven: Yale University Press, 1997), p. 178.
16. Author's interviews with 'Sara', 06/03/01 and 09/03/01. Sara is a 26-year-old youth worker, based in Aubervilliers. She was brought to Aubervilliers at the age of six by her Moroccan parents.
17. B. Anderson, *Imagined Communities: Reflections on the Origin and Spread of Nationalism* (London: Verso, 1991).
18. N. G. Souilamas, *Des 'beurettes' aux descendants d'immigrants nord-africains* (Paris: Grasset & Fasquelle, 2000), pp. 99–100.
19. Author's interview with 'Hala' and 'Mona', 18/05/01.
20. Author's interview with 'Fawzia', 18/04/01.
21. Anderson, *Imagined Communities*.
22. Author's interview with 'Touran', 22/03/01. 'Me, simply as a young person because the young people here, there are French people in my neighbourhood who are slogging away just as much as me [...] it's clear so, no, as a young person, neither as Maghrebi origin, nor as a Muslim [...] just as a young person...'.
23. Author's interview with 'Abdel Majid', 'Ahmed' and 'Maliha', 22/05/01.
24. D. Lapeyronnie, 'De l'altérité à la différence. L'identité, facteur d'intégration ou de repli?', in P. Dewitte (ed.), *Immigration et intégration, l'état des savoirs* (Paris: La Découverte et Syros, 1999), p. 257.
25. Interview with 'Sara', 06/03/01.
26. N. Kiwan, 'The Citizen and the Subject', in A. Cole and G. Raymond (eds), *Redefining the French Republic* (Manchester: Manchester University Press, 2006), pp. 97–116.
27. M. Barthélémy cites J.-P. Martin, 'A la recherche d'un modèle associatif laïc', *La revue de l'économie sociale*, April (1988), p. 137, in *Associations: un nouvel âge de participation?* (Paris: Presses de la Fondation Nationale des Sciences Politiques, 2000).
28. A. Jazouli, *Une saison en banlieue: courants et prospectives dans les quartiers populaires* (Paris: Plon, 1995).
29. Details on damage caused during the riots are from *Aubermensuel Supplément au no.155, novembre 2005*, p. 4. Well before the riots of the autumn, Aubervilliers had already been the theatre for urban unrest following the death of a young man trying to escape the Brigade anti-criminalité on 1 April 2005. Following his death, riots broke out and youths were caught up in confrontations with the police for a number of nights. Cars and a local commercial depot were burnt.
30. M. Kokoreff, P. Barron and O. Steinauer, *Enquêtes dur les violences urbaines: comprendre les émeutes de novembre 2005, l'exemple de Saint-Denis* (Paris: Centre d'analyse stratégique, Département Institutions et Société, novembre 2006). Report presented to the Prime Minister.
31. D. Lapeyronnie, 'Révolte primitive dans les banlieues françaises. Essai sur les émeutes de l'automne 2005', *Déviance et Société*, 304 (2006).

32. See L. Muchielli and A. Aït Omar, 'Introduction générale', in L. Muchielli and V. Le Goaziou (eds), *Quand les banlieues brûlent...Retour sur les émeutes de novembre 2005* (Paris: Editions La Découvrte, 2006), p. 19.
33. See A. Bozzo, 'Islam et République: une longue histoire de méfiance', in P. Blanchard, N. Bancel and S. Lemaire (eds), *La Fracture coloniale: la société française au prisme de l'héritage colonial* (Paris: Editions La Découverte, 2005), pp. 75–82 for an interesting discussion on the historical experience of the French Republic's relationship with Islam, particularly in colonial Algeria. Bozzo argues that this mode of dealing with Islam is quite clearly echoed in France today. On the declining numbers of pupils wearing conspicuous religious symbols, see Ministère de l'éducation nationale de l'enseignement supérieur et de la recherche, *Application de La Loi du 15 mars 2004 sur le port des signes religieux ostensibles dans les établissements d'enseignement publics,* Rapport à monsieur le ministre de l'éducation nationale de l'enseignement supérieur et de la recherche. Rapporteur Hanifa Chérifi, juillet 2005, pp. 41–6.
34. See *Appel du 19 janvier 2005*, www.indigenes-republique.org.

Select bibliography

Anderson, B., *Imagined Communities: Reflections on the Origin and Spread of Nationalism*, rev. edn (London: Verso, 1991).
Barthélémy, M., *Associations: un nouvel âge de participation?* (Paris: Presses de la Fondation Nationale des Sciences Politiques, 2000).
Blanchard, P., Bancel, N. and Lemaire, S. (eds), *La Fracture coloniale: la société française au prisme de l'héritage colonial* (Paris: Editions La Découverte, 2005).
Cole, A. and Raymond, G. (eds), *Redefining the French Republic* (Manchester: Manchester University Press, 2006).
Dubet, F., *La Galère: jeunes en survie* (Paris: Fayard, 1997).
Guénif Souilamas, N., *Des 'beurettes' aux descendants d'immigrants nord-africains* (Paris: Grasset & Fasquelle, 2000).
Jazouli, A., *Une saison en banlieue: courants et prospectives dans les quartiers populaires* (Paris: Plon, 1995).
Dewitte, P. (ed.), *Immigration et intégration, l'état des savoirs* (Paris: La Découverte et Syros, 1999).
Lepoutre, D., *Coeur de banlieue: codes, rites et langages* (Paris: Odile Jacob, 2001).
Muchielli, L. and Le Goaziou, V. (eds), *Quand les banlieues brûlent ... Retour sur les émeutes de novembre 2005* (Paris: Editions La Découverte, 2006).
Simmel, G., *Essays on Religion*, ed. and trans. by H.J. Helle in collaboration with L. Nieder (New Haven: Yale University Press, 1997).
Wieviorka, M., *La Différence culturelle: une reformulation des débats* (Paris: Balland, 2001).

6
Converging at Last? France, Britain and their Minorities

Vincent Latour

Introduction

Both the British and the French approaches to ethnic diversity have been the targets of mutual caricatures (or at least, oversimplifications) as both countries have developed over the years a quite cynical view of each other's management of immigration and of the subsequent shift to a multiethnic, multiracial and multi-faith society. The French are usually very dismissive of what they perceive as the differentialist, community-based, British approach whereas the British are very critical of the French universalist one, which they perceive as downright assimilationist. Although such views are somewhat caricatured, they are justified to a certain extent and in any case, testify to the diverging approaches that were set up in both countries as a result of mass, post-war, colonial immigration. While their lines have so far been diverging, to say the least, it seems that the problems faced by both countries have been converging. Indeed, the French can no longer claim that religious or ethnic divisions are triggered by a community-based management of race relations, as they themselves are faced with unprecedented religious tensions: violation of Muslim, Jewish and Christian cemeteries, agitation over a law reasserting the banning of outward display of religious affiliation in state schools,[1] large-scale riots throughout the country in the *banlieues* (i.e. those outer suburbs mostly inhabited by people of immigrant descent) during the autumn of 2005 and so on.

As for the British, they can no longer dismiss integration as a French anomaly, as long-held beliefs in the virtues of 'unity in diversity' are increasingly being questioned. The official objective pursued by the British government now seems to be 'to integrate all communities in a multicultural framework', as recommended by the Community Cohesion

Panel headed by Ted Cantle in *The End of Parallel Lives?*,[2] a report released in 2004. More recently, Tony Blair said in what has been referred to as his 'multiculturalism speech', that Britain had to find 'the right balance between integration and diversity'.[3] Likewise, the Islamic veil controversy triggered by Jack Straw in September 2006 has shown the scope of the change in process and that such issues continued to create tension.

In recent years, both France and Britain have been trying to adjust their long-established approaches to ethnic diversity to new challenges and issues threatening national unity and cohesion. Unsurprisingly, the routes taken by both countries are, at least superficially, once more diverging. What is surprising, however, is that we are witnessing some sort of 'inverted convergence', in the sense that the British seem to turn to characteristics that have so far been associated with the French republican model, whereas France, at least at first glance, seems to be tempted to redefine its national model through methods inspired by the British system and more generally by other countries whose official policy has been based more or less literally on multiculturalism. First, I will show to what extent the French and the British approaches to ethnic, racial and religious diversity have diverged until now. In my second point, I will try to establish that despite their distinct orientations, both countries are currently confronted with similar issues. Then, in the rest of this chapter, I will discuss the relevance of the concept of 'inverted convergence' mentioned earlier. In order to illustrate the 'British side' of this chapter I will refer to research, past and present, that I have been pursuing on minorities and race relations in Bristol, which, in many ways, may be regarded as a microcosm of the wider society.

Diverging traditions

What is known as the 'British model' of race relations (some go even so far as to talk of a British exception) partly rests on the fact that the apparent generosity of post-war migratory policies gave birth to what was to be later known as 'the multicultural society'. After the independence of India (1947), a distinction was established between British subjects from the UK and its colonies and Commonwealth citizens. However, under the 1948 British Nationality Act, British citizenship was granted to all Commonwealth citizens. Despite previous restrictions, black (or at least, non-white) British subjects were legally entitled to settle in Britain, although, unofficially, preference was given to white immigration. This so-called generosity was short-lived. Fourteen years later, the 1962 Commonwealth Immigrants Act restricted New Commonwealth immigration. That trend has never since been reversed. Yet the British Nationality Act was a real departure from wartime legislation. Indeed, in 1945 the Aliens legislation still formed the basis of the entry of non-British subjects.

The second element upon which rests what is known as the British model also has to do (though indirectly) with the British Nationality Act. In 1965, the Labour government was well aware of widespread racial discrimination. Harold Wilson and his fellow Labourites, who had become converted to immigration restrictions, knew that racial discrimination, especially in employment and housing, would become an increasingly controversial political issue. In fact, in view of the surrounding anti-black hysteria, the underlying problem was the question of the future of race relations at a time when race riots were developing across the Atlantic (e.g. the Watts riot in Los Angeles in 1964). Fears of a potential evolution along American lines (a fear that had existed since the Notting Hill and Nottingham riots, in 1958) prompted the successive Wilson governments to take action: the Race Relations Act 1965 was therefore passed. Significantly, the Act came into force on 8 December 1965, i.e. two and a half months after Executive Order 11246 first enforced Affirmative Action in the US. The 1965 Act paved the way for more coercive legislation (also passed under Labour rule), the 1968 and 1976 Race Relations Acts, the latter creating the Commission for Racial Equality.

Immigration restrictions found themselves combined with integration measures, a strategy frequently referred to as 'the dual interventionist strategy', best summed up by Roy Hattersley's famous observation in 1965: 'Integration without control is impossible, but control without integration is indefensible.'[4] Likewise, the aim of the Local Government Act (1966) and of the Urban Programme (1968) was to relieve deprived inner-city areas (where most ethnic minority people were concentrated) through central government funding.

Some local authorities showed similar determination in dealing with racial issues. In 1958, Bristol City Council hired a welfare advisory officer whose aim was 'to assist coloured immigrants with their adjustment problems'.[5] When that post was created, there were only some 4000 New Commonwealth immigrants in the Bristol area (i.e. roughly 1 per cent of the population), as against just over 1000 in 1951.[6] That officer was appointed at a time when the national political debate started shifting from immigration to the emergence of a multicultural and multiracial society, just after the Notting Hill and Nottingham riots, which brought racial tensions to the forefront of the news and of the political debate.

The British approach came in sharp contrast with the migratory policies of continental countries. Indeed, while Britain was paving the way for the advent of a multiracial society, France perceived immigration in purely economic terms, thus overlooking its social and political dimensions. Michel Wieviorka holds that during the *trente glorieuses* (the three decades of economic expansion and full employment that followed the Second World War), immigrants were kept at a distance by French society. Somehow that situation suited many of them, who perceived their presence in France as temporary. To Wieviorka, immigrants were socially integrated through work but were excluded as regards other aspects of public and political life. The irony was that two decades or so later, in the post-industrial age, their French-born sons and daughters found themselves in the opposite situation. On the one hand, unlike their parents, they were integrated from the political point of view, as they were full-fledged French citizens. On the other hand, they were excluded socially, as they were far more likely to be unemployed than the general population, notably due to racial discrimination.[7]

A similar approach prevailed in Germany, where a *Gastarbeiter* policy was set up. In Britain, unlike in France, immigrants had citizenship rights and therefore, 'the primary focus of the debate about equality had to be on combating racial and ethnic discrimination'.[8]

Unlike Britain, France set up no specific race relations legislation. Cases of racial discrimination were to be tackled through the normal courts. In France, in addition to the 1789 universalist ideals that stated that the only relevant distinction to be made was between French nationals (who had citizenship rights) and non-French nationals (who did not have such rights), the experience of Nazi occupation and of the collaborationist Vichy regime may partly explain the reluctance to acknowledge the existence of racial divisions or indeed, even to use the term 'race'. Paradoxically, as rightly emphasised by John Rex, the problems encountered by immigrants in France have been frequently explained by the racism of majority groups.[9] Though egalitarian in essence, universalist republican ideals meant that in the context of massive post-war immigration and of the emergence of a culturally diverse population, it became difficult to acknowledge cultural differences, which, it was thought, could denote inequality. The main challenge for French people advocating multiculturalism (such as political activists, academics) was therefore to show that recognition of cultural diversity did not necessarily endanger the institutions meant to ensure equality between individuals.[10] That dilemma is still very topical.

Despite these distinct approaches, it seems that Britain and France are now confronted with similar issues, namely a crisis of their integration models. Through reference to my research in Bristol, I will now attempt to expose these contemporary problems.

The Bristol experience

I started my research on race relations in Bristol in the mid-1990s, when I went to work there as a French assistant. Race relations in Bristol have received comparatively little academic attention, above all because Bristol's ethnic minority population is smaller than that of many other cities. Yet the latest census reveals that the size of Bristol's BME (black and minority ethnic) population has risen from 5.13 per cent in 1991 to 8.2 per cent in 2001. That percentage is below the average for England and Wales (9.08 per cent) but above the British average (7.6 per cent).[11]

This growth is chiefly due to the fact that the ethnic minorities continue to be characterised by a higher birth rate than the rest of the population. When the latest census was taken, in 2001, a national survey carried out by the Office for National Statistics (ONS) showed that Britain's ethnic minorities grew at 15 times the rate of the white population. Unsurprisingly, the fastest-growing groups were the most recently settled groups. Bangladeshis, for instance, many of whom came in the 1970s and 1980s, had a much higher birth rate than Pakistanis and above all Indians, whose immigration took place mostly in the 1950s and 1960s. The same study revealed equally significantly that the fastest-growing group of all was the 'black mixed' category, growing at 49 per cent, as against 1 per cent for the white population,[12] thus testifying to an increasing trend towards exogamy, chiefly between Britain's black and white populations, despite evidence of marginal intermarriage between, for example, blacks and Asians. In any case, despite the growth in the ethnic minority population, Bristol's overall population has stagnated or indeed, slightly decreased over the last five decades, passing from 402,657 inhabitants in 1951, to an estimated 398,300 inhabitants in mid-2005 (England's sixth largest city).[13] Between 1991 and 2001 alone, Bristol lost some 12,000 inhabitants, i.e. roughly a 3 per cent drop. By comparison, Toulouse, a French city relatively comparable in size, has been gaining an average 12,000 inhabitants per annum over the last decade, passing from 390,301 inhabitants in 1999 to 431,500 in 2004, thus becoming France's fourth largest city. However, it now seems that population loss is no longer an issue for Bristol, considering that the mid-2005 estimates revealed an increase by 8300 people compared with the 2001 figures.

Bristol's ethnic minority population is young. Over 50 per cent of Indians, Pakistanis and Bangladeshis are under 25, as against roughly 30 per cent for white Europeans. The Equalities Audit 2005 issued by Bristol City Council shows that 21.2 per cent of all pupils from reception class to year 11 in Bristol's state schools are BME pupils,[14] as against 20 per cent in the rest of the country.[15] A closer scrutiny of the census results in the Bristol area reveals that the socio-economic and educational gap between some sections of the ethnic minorities and the white population is widening. The unemployment figures revealed by the latest census are particularly telling. In 2001, the unemployment rate for the overall population was 3.1 per cent in Bristol, as against 3.2 per cent in the rest of the country.[16] That all-time low unemployment conceals the gap between white and black Bristolians and also between the various ethnic groups themselves. Thus, a detailed analysis of the census shows that Indians, Pakistanis, Bangladeshis and Afro-Caribbeans, i.e. Bristol's four main ethnic groups, are far more likely to be unemployed than the overall population. With a 6 per cent unemployment rate, Indians, who are often regarded as the best economically integrated group, are twice as likely to be out of work as the general population.

The situation is much worse for Pakistanis and Afro-Caribbeans (11 per cent), and worse still for Bangladeshis, 13 per cent of whom are unemployed, i.e. roughly three times the Bristol average for the April 2005–March 2006 period. Likewise, Bangladeshis are three times as likely as the rest of the population to be employed only part-time (35 per cent). These results are very much in line with the nationwide average.

Similarly, the conclusions reached by the latest Equalities Audit issued by the Bristol City Council's Department of Education and Lifelong Learning indicate that most ethnic minority groups suffer educational disadvantages:

> Pupils from the Black African ethnic group had the lowest results in every subject as well as for boys and girls compared with other ethnic groups. The attainment of Black Caribbean pupils in Reading and Writing was also of concern. Generally, children from Black or Asian groups did not do as well as the citywide average. All of the Mixed White and Asian and Chinese pupils performed well, compared to all of the pupils as a whole [...]To summarise, Black and minority ethnic pupils as a group had lower attainment than non-BME pupils at the

benchmark of Level 2+ at Key Stage 1 by 7.9 per cent in Reading, 8.64 per cent in Writing and 8.1 per cent in Maths. Particular issues impacting on attainment may be language acquisition for pupils with EAL, and mobility within Early Years and at KS1.[17]

Segregation, in all its forms, is also an issue in Bristol. The latest census indicates that just like in the rest of the country, BME groups in Bristol are very unevenly distributed. For example, in Ashley, which is part of St Paul's, 67 per cent of the population is white, as against 96.2 per cent in Hartcliffe or Stockwood.

More worrying still is the fact that there seems to be greater segregation in schools than in the neighbourhoods themselves. Indeed, the Equalities Audit shows that the percentage of white British pupils in the wards with a sizeable BME population is much smaller than the percentage of whites in the area as a whole and things seem to have worsened in recent years. For example, in Ashley, where 67 per cent of the population is white, the percentage of white British pupils is 36.9 per cent (as against 39.1 per cent in 2004). In other areas the gap is equally dramatic. In Easton, for example, 71.3 per cent of the population is white, compared with 40.8 per cent of the pupils attending school in the area (43 per cent in 2004). In Lawrence Hill, where most of Easton actually is, 64.2 per cent of the population is white, as against a mere 28.3 per cent in the local schools (30.4 per cent in 2004).[18]

The socio-economic disadvantage suffered by many inner-city ethnic minority families means that, although some degree of choice has existed since the Education Reform Act (1988) they are either unable to send their children to state schools that enjoy a better reputation, or merely unaware that they can do so. As a result, the schools situated in the inner-city areas find themselves segregated along social and ethnic lines, which fosters a sense of 'separateness'. Although there is disagreement over this issue, recent academic research carried out at the University of Bristol suggests that increasing the scope for 'choice' (a recurring theme in the British political debate over recent years) could lead in fact not to more diverse communities but to more segregated schools.[19] In recent years some of the local schools attended by children from the inner-city areas mentioned above have undergone considerable change. The school formerly known as Saint George Community School had a multi-million pound rebuild and became the new City Academy in 2003, the first such school in the South West. Similarly Fairfield High in the Montpellier area (near St Paul's) has doubled its capacity (it now has places for 1080 pupils as against 500 previously) and relocated to a brand new building, 'likened to an ocean-going liner and it is embarking on a voyage of change as well as expanding',[20] as somewhat pompously put by Bristol City Council. Whether such entirely laudable initiatives will persuade parents from other areas to send their children to these schools and to make them more socio-economically and ethnically diverse remains to be seen. In any case, I found that sense of 'separateness' particularly acute both in Saint Paul's and Easton when doing fieldwork there. Indeed, many voluntary organisations in Easton, including some involved in the fight against racism, struck me as being largely fragmented along ethnic or religious lines. Most of the organisations that claim to be non-confessional are actually meant for strictly defined religious groups. The term 'Asian', a potentially ecumenical term which appears in the names of some supposedly non-confessional organisations, means almost always 'Sikh', 'Hindu', 'Indian', 'Pakistani', 'Muslim' or 'Christian'.

Easton Asian Women's Group was one of the community organisations I surveyed in Easton. During an interview, this group's coordinator, Jasbir, assured me that her organisation was not in any way segmented along religious or ethnic lines:

> Our organization includes all Asian women, and Chinese women, that is Muslims, Sikhs, Christians, any Asian religion, any religion. We need to network with other women's groups, in order to tell them about services and projects that we have in Easton. Talking to women of other organizations highlights the needs of women.[21]

However, in spite of that generous and open discourse, I only met Sikh women in that group, significantly sheltered by a Sikh 'umbrella' organisation, the Sikh Resource Centre.

Such divisions are commonplace in Easton and are not confined to one specific community. In fact, the only comparatively diverse association I came across there was the Asian Health and Social Care Association, a day centre chiefly frequented by elderly East African Asians. Although most of the members of that club were Hindus, there also were some Sikhs and a few Muslims. Significantly, the salaried coordinator of that group was Salim, a Muslim from Uganda. It seemed, indeed, that what brought these people together was the status (possibly partly conferred by their British nationality) that they shared in colonial Kenya or Uganda prior to their expulsion, which occurred in the late 1960s and early 1970s.

The organisations I surveyed in St Paul's seemed for the most part unable, or even unwilling, to interact as their Easton counterparts. Indeed, Afro-Caribbeans from Jamaica and Barbados, for example, seemed to frequent distinct organisations. Even potential rallying events, such as the Saint Paul's carnival, are not actually cohesive, as pointed out by Cathie, who both works and lives in Easton: 'Big organisations aren't very co-operative. They have a very regional, if not parochial focus. They are interested in getting grants for themselves and claim to be representative. The Carnival has also been very insular.'[22] Those divisions are aggravated by the fact that community organisations compete for resources, which have become increasingly scarce since the early 1990s as successive governments, both Conservative and Labour, have favoured the more 'professional' and business-minded organisations.

This rivalry is also true of Somali and Afro-Caribbean organisations. Somalis, many of whom have come to Bristol as refugees or asylum seekers since the fiasco of the UN-led operation Restore Hope, have settled mostly in Saint Paul's. They try to obtain subsidies through their community organisations. Unsurprisingly, these demands clash with those that emanate from the Afro-Caribbean organisations, which exacerbates the squabbling over the meagre resources given by the council and the tensions between groups that are very different culturally:

> The relationship between the Somali community and Afro-Caribbeans is one of the main issues locally at the moment. There is a racial dimension to that conflict. The two communities are squabbling over playgrounds, resources etc. That could – and probably will – lead to conflict sooner or later. It's far more of a problem than relations between whites and blacks. The Council sent most Somali refugees to St Paul's just because they are black, assuming they would get along with Afro-Caribbeans, whereas these communities have nothing in common. A lot of Somali organizations have emerged in recent years, many of which with very loosely defined aims and purposes, are delivering no services. The Council has had to make those groups understand that they have to deliver services.[23]

Are the segmentation of the Asian or Caribbean community organisations along ethnic or religious lines and more generally, intercommunity tensions, confined to Bristol? Actually, they seem to be the consequences of the British multiculturalist approach, which has tolerated or even encouraged the irruption of cultural demands in the public sphere. Wieviorka argues that one of the perverse effects of multiculturalism is that groups that are prone to benefit from policies of cultural recognition tend to reject interculturality (notably through opposition to exogamy), as it is a way for them to obtain material or token advantages. To Wieviorka, in any given ethnic community, some particular policies benefit chiefly the most affluent and influential members, enabling them to combine social advantages with cultural particularisms, thus 'circulating comfortably but possibly unfairly between their culture and the advantages that they are offered by the globalized economy in which they participate'.[24] Similar conclusions are reached by another leading French sociologist, Didier Lapeyronnie, in his enlightening comparative analysis of the management of population diversity on both sides of the Channel. He terms community leaders an 'intermediate milieu' that tends to consider community members merely as a 'clientele'.[25]

Such community organisations first struck me as having above all a particularist agenda, owing to their fragmentation and to their cultural demands, especially those emanating from Easton-based Muslim organisations, which actively campaigned for local issues, such as the opening of a Muslim school in Bristol (the nearest was in Gloucester until Andalusia Academy, 'Bristol's first full time Islamic School',[26] opened in Saint Paul's in September 2005), or for national issues, such as the recognition of British Muslims as an ethnic group. However, financial or economic considerations (the question of subsidies and of the perpetuation of jobs within the 'ethnic' voluntary sector) were central. They seemed to be an end in themselves and to play an even greater role than demands for cultural or religious recognition. These findings seem to support Wieviorka's view that socio-economic and cultural (in the broad acceptation of this term) demands are frequently intertwined, which means that economic demands may be mistaken for cultural ones. In fact, Wieviorka suggests that 'culture' or indeed religion may be put forward to formulate socio-economic demands.[27] In his 'multiculturalism speech' that he delivered in December 2006, Tony Blair recognised that public subsidies had so far been granted to ethnic organisations somewhat naively and had fostered divisions:

> First, we need to use the grants we give to community racial and religious groups to promote integration as well as help distinctive cultural identity [...] We wanted to be hospitable to new groups. We wanted, rightly, to extend a welcome and did so by offering public money to entrench their cultural presence. Money was too often

freely awarded to groups that were tightly bonded around religious, racial or ethnic identities. In the future, we will assess bids from groups of any ethnicity or any religious denomination, also against a test, where appropriate, of promoting community cohesion and integration.[28]

France is not devoid of such examples of deprivation and segregation. It would be really interesting to compare the educational achievement of ethnic minority pupils in Britain with that of their counterparts in France, but ethnic monitoring is illegal in France, where the expression 'ethnic minorities' is unheard of and where the notion of communitarianism (frequently associated with the phrase 'à l'anglo-saxonne') is practically an insult. The three-week-long riots that shook the Republic in October and November 2005 prompted the French government to consider the option of resorting to anti-discriminatory tools such as anonymous CVs, which have been the norm for almost two decades in the UK. Such a minimalist option sufficed to spark off a furious debate and Monsieur de Villepin's right-of-centre government eventually backed down, although it had promised after the crisis in the *banlieues* that such a measure would quickly be implemented. Although a pilot survey was carried out in a number of big corporations in 2004–5 under the aegis of the Institut National des Etudes Démographiques (the National Institute of Demographic Studies), the very fact of carrying out ethnic monitoring or at least to mention ethnic origins in population censuses is extremely controversial. It is generally admitted, however, that such a step would be necessary first to highlight and then address issues of ethnic segregation and deprivation. Cynics have frequently argued that French authorities have been reluctant to set up ethnic monitoring lest it should reveal the full extent of ethnic segregation in republican France. In October 2006, a conference was organised by the Centre d'Analyse Stratégique (the Centre of Strategic Analysis, a public research institute which advises the Prime Minister), notably in order to look into the way other Western countries have dealt with such issues.[29] *Le Monde*, France's leading quality left-of-centre newspaper, underlined the irony of a conference entitled 'Statistiques ethniques', in a country where 'there are officially no Blacks, no Arabs, no Asians, at least in the eyes of the law'.[30]

Still, it is generally admitted that pupils of North African origin, for example, especially those with foreign-born parents or foreign-born themselves, suffer educational disadvantage. As for segregation in schools, it is commonplace, especially in big urban or suburban centres, as recently evidenced by Georges Felouzis, a sociologist who owing to the absence of ethnic monitoring in France, based himself upon first names and the place of birth of parents to demonstrate that some *collèges* (secondary schools, from the equivalent of year 7 to year 10) in the Bordeaux area were more segregated along ethnic than along social lines. He goes so far as to call six of them 'ghettos'. Indeed, Felouzis argues that it would require sending 90 per cent of pupils of North African or African descent to different schools for them to be evenly distributed in the Aquitaine region, that is the region whose capital city is Bordeaux.[31]

Likewise, no data are available for unemployment, but there is widespread evidence of non-white people being disadvantaged or discriminated against, just as in housing. Those hitherto ignored issues (that have remained virtually unaddressed so far) came to the surface only recently, during and after the 2005 crisis in the *banlieues*. Prior to then, the issue was carefully avoided by the authorities. When France won the World Cup in 1998, 'la France black-blanc-beur'[32] epitomised by Zinedine Zidane was extolled, which meant that issues of integration and racial discrimination were silenced or altogether ignored for a few years.

In addition to these socio-economic issues, religious and ethnic tensions have been on the rise in France, as shown in the agitation over the adoption and implementation of the law on outward signs of religious affiliation in schools, in the many cases of profanation perpetrated against Jewish, Muslim and Christian cemeteries or places of worship, or indeed the assaults on some Jewish or Muslim clerics. The sense of 'separateness' has also been palpable in some Paris suburbs where the mayors have yielded to pressure from Jewish and Muslim religious organisations and have provided 'female-only' access to public swimming pools. So, although it would be simplistic to say that the situation of both countries is identical, it is merely stating the obvious to argue that both of them are confronted with symptoms that betray a crisis of their integration models.

Lately, to respond to such challenges, both countries have been convinced, or at least tempted, to review their handling of issues related to racial or religious minorities, some of those proposals being real departures from past policies or indeed, national traditions. Yet there is a sense in which the extent of the intended reform is much greater in the UK than in France. I will now try to give some examples of those intended reforms, as well as examine the relevance of the comparison between the two countries in this particular regard.

Converging realities?

Until recently, the determination of the British in terms of fighting racism was in sharp contrast to their laissez-faire attitude towards managing the diversity of the population. The word 'integration' was somewhat taboo, and in some cases was considered as altogether racist. That is now changing. Indeed, the British government seems to take a much more holistic and comprehensive approach than in the past, as shown, for example, in the merger of the Commission for Racial Equality (CRE) with other anti-discrimination bodies into a Commission for Equality and Human Rights (CEHR) headed by Trevor Phillips, former chair of the CRE. The CEHR will come into being in October 2007 as a result of the implementation of the Equality Act (2006). The CRE should disappear as a distinct entity in April 2009. Its new chair, Kay Hampton, has however expressed the wish to create a new NGO specialising in racial discrimination that could cooperate with the newly merged commission.

While the attacks of 7 July 2005 certainly accelerated the process, the project of moving towards a single anti-discriminatory body had actually long been on the government's agenda, as shown in the following statement made by Patricia Hewitt, the then Trade and Industry Secretary, one year prior to the London bomb attacks:

> We are fully committed to the creation of a single equality and human rights commission, which we believe will help create a more equal and cohesive society. We have made it clear to the CRE and other stakeholders that we want to work with them on both the timescale and the work of the body.[33]

People working at Bristol Racial Equality Council expressed concern when I met them in August 2004, as that proposed reform seemed to threaten the very existence of their organisation. The reform is merely one facet of the government's determination to enhance 'community cohesion', as well as a sense of common citizenship, as recommended as early as 2004 in the report drafted by the Community Cohesion Panel chaired by Ted Cantle.[34] It seems that the expression 'community cohesion' acts as a euphemism for the term 'integration', which, over the past two decades, has had negative connotations in the UK. Yet politicians now use that word, although they usually make sure it is presented positively and not mistaken for what is often perceived as French-style assimilation. Such is the case of Tony Blair, who best summed up the new British approach in the speech that he delivered under the aegis of the Runnymede Trust on 8 December 2006: 'The right to be different. The duty to integrate. That is what being British means. And neither racists nor extremists should be allowed to destroy it.'[35]

The notion of 'community cohesion' and the pursuit of integration in a multicultural framework have actually been on the government's agenda since the riots that broke out in 2001 in Oldham, Bradford and other cities. The Ouseley Report, entitled *Community Pride, Not Prejudice*, showed that separateness or indeed, self-segregation was an issue in some cities: 'Different communities seek to protect their identities and cultures by discouraging and avoiding contact with other communities and institutions. Bradford is the ultimate challenge to race relations in Britain.'[36] All the inquiries into those riots criticised the various local authorities for turning a blind eye to cases of self-segregation or indeed, for fanning the flames of division by empowering excessively some community leaders. The Cantle panel took those remarks into account. The report, *The End of Parallel Lives?*, stresses that both central and local governments should take the lead in promoting community cohesion.

The report also emphasised the need to introduce new citizenship ceremonies. They should be extended to all 18-year-olds with the aim of developing mutual commitments. The government followed that advice and set up such ceremonies, the first of which occurred in London on 26 February 2004, in the presence of David Blunkett, the then Home Secretary, and Prince Charles.[37] Citizenship education, which the Blair government has tried to promote, should be reviewed and extended, like the *éducation civique* classes, a long-established component of French primary and secondary education. More recently, in December 2006, when Tony Blair delivered what has been referred to as his 'multiculturalism speech', he emphasised the role of citizenship education, arguing that 'the national curriculum needs to stress integration rather than separation'.

What is striking in Britain is the scope of the consensus on the necessity of both reforming the system and of mending attitudes as well as the recognition by politicians or indeed statesmen of past naivety in public policies towards population diversity management. 'In a sense, very good intentions got the better of us', Tony Blair recognised in his Runnymede Trust speech. Similarly long-established race equality strategies (e.g. positive discrimination and quotas) have recently come under attack, including among sections of the ethnic minorities (e.g. in the Metropolitan Police, London).[38] Other examples could be given, such as the fact the ethnic minorities are not a specific target population of the New Deal for Employment despite their specific needs (although it is easily understandable that the extreme diversity of the minorities would make it simply impossible to devise a single, comprehensive strategy for all of them). Britain seems therefore to be gradually moving away from its traditional approach and to adopt some characteristics that may be said to have been previously associated with French universalism.

France, conversely, seems somehow to be moving away from its rigid republican approach. Although religious neutrality remains more than ever the official rule, notably in schools, France is beginning, at long last, to come to terms with its multicultural dimension. This trend is palpable, among other examples, in the belated creation of the Conseil Français du Culte Musulman (the French Council for the Muslim Faith), a representative body for Islam which appeared in 2003 (although the initial project had been formulated in 1999, while the socialist Lionel Jospin was in office). Backed by the government, officials from that body went to Iraq during the summer of 2004 to try to obtain the release of the two French journalists who had been held as hostages there.

Multicultural education, one of the great merits of the British approach, was until recently totally unheard of in France. Separation between Church and state meant that it was very difficult to deal with religious matters in state schools. Since the beginning of the 2004 school year, all pupils attending *collège* have been given a dictionary of religions (Christianity, Islam, Judaism and Buddhism). They are now taught more than in the past about the history of religions as part of the above-mentioned *éducation civique* classes. Another project that has been mentioned in government circles is to put a few Muslim and Jewish festivals on an equal footing with Roman Catholic ones, including as regards bank holidays. Likewise, the creation of the HALDE (Haute Autorité de Lutte contre les Discriminations et pour l'Egalité) in 2005, a public anti-discriminatory body comparable to the Commission for Equality and Human Rights, testifies to that change. The above-mentioned reforms have generally been accepted and perceived as fair, though long overdue.

Some other initiatives or projects, however, have been much more controversial and have caused a great deal of alarm. For example, Nicolas Sarkozy, the Minister of the Interior, appointed a *préfet* of North African descent, whom he presented as a *préfet musulman* (i.e. a Muslim prefect). Many people, both in the majority and the opposition, were shocked, obviously not because the prefect was Muslim, but simply because it is very unlike the republican tradition to pigeonhole people according to their religious affiliation. The appointment of that civil servant was much publicised, although there had been quite a few non-Christian prefects in the past, among whom were several Muslims. Similarly, the Minister of the Interior, Nicolas Sarkozy, said on several occasions that he was in favour of setting up race equality strategies (e.g. positive discrimination and quotas) so as to better reflect the ethnic diversity of France. Such initiatives are not strictly associated with one particular political party. The possibility of introducing quotas was mentioned before 2002 by the Socialist government and was equally controversial then, although it was supported by some Socialist leaders, such as Jack Lang or Martine Aubry.

It can therefore be said that the comparison between recent, actual or proposed reforms in France and Britain should not be overstated. What is true is that both countries are in the process of altering their long-established approaches to ethnic, racial and religious diversity, but while Britain seems to be trying to devise an altogether new orientation around 'the duty to integrate' (an underlying message since 9/11 and 7/7, which became very explicit in Tony Blair's Runnymede Trust speech), it seems that France is merely updating, at long last, its own approach, as it is eventually coming to terms with its multicultural dimension. That does not mean, however, that there is no support among some politicians, community leaders or members of minority groups for the introduction of positive discrimination measures, for example, although the pilot survey carried out in several corporations by the INED (the National Institute of Demographic Studies) has revealed that French people, including those of African or North African descent, are highly suspicious of the very notion of ethnic monitoring,[39] a possible indication that republican principles are endorsed even by those who France is reluctant to recognise as distinct citizens.

Conclusion

Some issues related to minority groups are definitely converging in France and Britain, just as they are converging in most multicultural, multiracial and multi-faith Western countries in today's post-9/11 world. It is, however, doubtful that both countries are actually 'converging', even in an inverted way. In any case, there is so much opposition to 'radical' race relations reforms in France, both inside and outside Parliament, and so much attachment to republican ideals, that any 'Big Bang' evolution along multiculturalist lines is highly unlikely in the near future. Any country committed to a sincere redefinition of its approach to cultural and religious diversity would no doubt have avoided the controversy and complications caused by passing a new law limiting the outward display of religious affiliation in its schools and would have taken immediate and concrete action after the 2005 riots instead of sticking to its usual, low-key treatment of such issues.

Notes

1. 'Loi n° 2004–228 du 15 mars 2004 encadrant, en application du principe de laïcité, le port de signes ou de tenues manifestant une appartenance religieuse dans les écoles, collèges et lycées publics.'
2. T. Cantle et al., *The End of Parallel Lives? The Report of the Community Cohesion Panel* (London: HMSO, 2004) p. 16.
3. *The Daily Telegraph*, 9 December 2006. http://www.telegraph.co.uk/news/main.jhtml?xml=/news/2006/12/08/ublair208.xml
4. J. Solomos, *Race and Racism in Britain* (London: Macmillan, 1993), p. 84.
5. A. H. Richmond, *Migration and Race Relations in an English City: a Study in Bristol* (London: OUP, 1973), p. 43.
6. Ibid., p. 41.
7. M. Wieviorka, *La différence* (Paris: Balland, 2001) p. 34.
8. J. Rex, 'Multiculturalism in Europe', in J. Hutchinson and A.D. Smith (eds), *Ethnicity* (Oxford: Oxford Readers, 1996), p. 242.
9. Ibid., p. 243.
10. Ibid.
11. No updates were available when this article was written in December 2006.
12. BBC News, "Ethnic Birth Rate Climbs', Friday, 21 September 2001. http://news.bbc.co.uk/1/hi/uk/1556901.stm
13. Bristol City Council, Statistics and Census Information. Population Estimates and Projections. http://www.bristol-city.gov.uk/ccm/content/Council-Democracy/Statistics-Census-Information/population-estimates-and-projections.en;jsessionid=1CF86F1A310DA87447F66828D611D76A
14. *Equalities Audit* (Bristol: Bristol City Council Department of Education and Lifelong Learning, 2005), 'Ethnicity Distribution', 10. http://www.bristol-cyps.org. uk/services/pdf/equalities_audit05.pdf
15. Department for Education and Skills, 'Pupil Characteristics and Class Sizes in Maintained Schools in England', January 2005. http:/www.dfes.gov.uk/rsgateway/DB/SFR/s000574/index/shtml
16. The general unemployment figures have since been updated: 4.4 per cent in Bristol over the April 2005–March 2006 period, as against 5 per cent in the UK as a whole. However, no updates were available for Bristol's ethnic minority unemployment when this chapter was completed in December 2006. Bristol City Council: Statistics and Census Information, Labour Market and Employment Statistics. http://www.bristol-city.gov.uk/ccm/content/Council-Democracy/Statistics-Census-Information/labour-market.en?#internalSection1

17. *Equalities Audit* (Bristol City Council, 2005), 'Black and Minority Ethnic Pupil Attainment', 24. http://www.bristol-cyps.org.uk/services/pdf/equalities_audit05.pdf
18. Ibid., 'Ethnicity Distribution by Ward', 10. http://www.bristol-cyps.org.uk/services/pdf/equalities_audit05.pdf
19. S. Burgess, B. McConnel, C. Propper and D. Wilson, 'Sorting and Choice in English Secondary Schools', Centre for Market and Public Organisation (CMPO), The University of Bristol, Discussion Paper No. 04/11 (Bristol: October 2004), 20. http://www.bris.ac.uk/Depts/CMPO/workingpapers/wp111.pdf
20. 'Three New-build Schools for Bristol'. http://www.bristol-city.gov.uk/ccm/content/press-releases/2006/apr/three-new-build-schools-for-bristol.en;jsessionid=42601FFD55B2D4A09453D452598EDBA6
21. Interview with Jasbir, Sikh Resource Centre, Easton, Monday 7 February 2000.
22. Interview with Cathie, Community Development Worker, Saint Paul's, Thursday 19 August 2004.
23. Interview with Cathie, Community Development Worker, St Paul's, Thursday 19 August 2004.
24. Wieviorka, *La différence*, p. 80 (my translation).
25. D. Lapeyronnie, *L'individu et les minorités: la France et la Grande-Bretagne face à leurs immigrés* (Paris: Presses Universitaires de France, 1993) pp. 284–5 (my translation).
26. Bristol Islamic Schools Trust. With 31 pupils when it opened in 2005 and 70 in 2006, the school has so far had a limited appeal. http://www.bist.org.uk/index.htm
27. Wieviorka, *La différence*, p. 33.
28. *The Daily Telegraph*, 9 December 2006. http://www.telegraph.co.uk/news/main.jhtml?xml=/news/2006/12/08/ublair208.xml
29. P. Y. Cusset, *Les statistiques 'ethniques': premiers éléments de cadrage*, Centre d'Analyse Stratégique, 'Colloque Statistiques Ethniques', 19 October 2006. www.strategie.gouv.fr/IMG/pdf/notecussetstatistiquesethniques.pdf
30. L. Van Eeckhout, 'Recensement *ethnique*: le débat français', *Le Monde*, 10 November 2006 (my translation).
31. G. Felouzis, 'Mixité urbaine et ségrégation ethnique dans les collèges français', in B. Jouve and A. G. Gagnon (eds), *Les métropoles au défi de la diversité culturelle* (Grenoble: PUG, 2006), p. 102.
32. 'Beur' is a slang word that designates a French-born person of North African origin.
33. P. Wintour, 'Battle Lines Drawn for Equality', *The Guardian*, 23 July 2004.
34. Cantle, *The End of Parallel Lives?*
35. *The Daily Telegraph*, 9 December 2006. http://www.telegraph.co.uk/news/main.jhtml?xml=/news/2006/12/08/ublair208.xml
36. H. Ouseley et al., *Community Pride not Prejudice: Making Diversity Work in Bradford* (Bradford: Bradford Vision, 2001), p. 10.
37. BBC News, 'First Citizenship Ceremony for UK', 26 February 2004. http://news.bbc.co.uk/1/hi/uk_politics/3487892.stm
38. 'White Police Claim Racism', *The Observer*, 22 August 2004.

39. C. Gabizon, 'Pas de catégories ethniques pour l'INED', *Le Figaro*, 1 July 2006. http://www.lefigaro.fr/france/20060701.FIG000000703_pas_de_categories_ethniques_pour_l_ined.html

Select bibliography

Cantle, T. et al., *The End of Parallel Lives? The Report of the Community Cohesion Panel* (London: HMSO, 2004).

Hutchinson, J. and Smith, A.D. (eds), *Ethnicity* (Oxford: Oxford Readers, 1996).

Jouve, B. and Gagnon, A.G. (eds), *Les métropoles au défi de la diversité culturelle* (Grenoble: PUG, 2006).

Lapeyronnie, D., *L'individu et les minorités: la France et la Grande-Bretagne face à leurs immigrés* (Paris: Presses Universitaires de France, 1993).

Ouseley, H. et al., *Community Pride not Prejudice: Making Diversity Work in Bradford* (Bradford: Bradford Vision, 2001).

Richmond, A.H., *Migration and Race Relations in an English City: a Study in Bristol* (London: OUP, 1973).

Solomos, J., *Race and Racism in Britain* (London: Macmillan, 1993).

Wieviorka, M., *La différence* (Paris: Balland, 2001).

7
Veiled Interventions in Pure Space: Honour, Shame and Embodied Struggles among Muslims in Britain and France[1]
Pnina Werbner

Introduction: the publicity of sexual intimacy

The paradox that sexual intimacy is neither intimate nor private but instead the subject of intense public deliberation, is rightly associated with the work of Michel Foucault. Standards of normalcy and deviancy, of the permitted and prohibited, can never, Foucault proposes, be the choice of individuals, but are subjected to normalising discourses and discursive practices by a range of modern professionals, even as these experts extol an end to sexual repression.[2]

Less widely acknowledged is Foucault's insight that in France at least, sexual freedoms came to assume a secondary symbolic load in relation to the nation and its liberation. Sexual freedom, like secularism itself, was elevated to sacred status. Hence, the constant tirade against sexual repression in France amounts, Foucault proposes, to a 'proclamation of a new day to come', an expression of the 'dream of a new city'.[3] In effect, it constitutes the horizon of republican freedom symbolically, despite the *de jure* and de facto exclusion of women in France until the post-war era from the freedoms accorded by the Revolution.[4] Indeed, in France this secondary symbolic load has precluded any serious public debate on some of the more pernicious effects on young girls of sexual promiscuity, pornography and the sex industry.

Foucault associates the publicity of intimacy with the advent of modernity. For social anthropologists it is, perhaps, a truism to argue that in pre-industrial societies too, including Asian and European peasant

117

societies, the publicity of sexual intimacy is a central factor of social control; indeed, public transgressions of sacred sexual taboos and norms in such societies inevitably lead to expulsion and murder, or at the very least to punitive legal consequences. This has been a salient feature of South Asian and Muslim societies in which notions of honour, shame and female sexual modesty have dominated group social relations between families and lineages, and continue to do so in the rural context. Veiling and purdah in these societies are perceived as external public symbols of female modesty and familial honour.

Like in the recent French 'headscarf affair', however, such practices have come to be symbolically loaded with new connotations and to stand diacritically for wider religious and national symbols within the context of migration and industrialisation. The meaning of veiling and, even, of sexual modesty, this chapter argues, is now so loaded with higher-order symbolic elaborations as to emit ambiguously a range of contradictory messages. These endow or deny agency to young South Asian and Muslim women in highly ambivalent ways.

Hence, the processes of higher-order symbolisation outlined here raise critical questions of authority: who has the authority to interpret the scriptures, in this case the Koran and ideas about individual liberty? Who has the right to determine the limits of modesty, or whom a young person should marry? As in the earlier confrontations in South Asia between Sufi saints and learned Muslim clerics,[5] the current contestation involves a range of actors claiming authoritative sacred knowledge: *ulama* of different tendencies, lay autodidact Islamists (among them are young women), modernists, reformists and secularists. The debates are international: Al Azhar in Egypt pronounces on veiling in France, Pakistan negotiates with the British state over forced marriages. Each of these hallowed public bodies invokes variously the authority of a text (the Koran), 'culture', 'religion', 'tradition', 'human rights', the 'community', the 'nation' or state law. In this debate what was once highly localised (a code of honour) has been *deterritorialised,* and the once self-evident reference to personal modesty obscured.

Feminists such as Nira Yuval-Davis have argued that all 'fundamentalist' (i.e. political) religious movements, whether Christian, Jewish, Hindu or Muslim, use the control of women's bodies symbolically, to assert a wider agenda of authoritarian political and cultural social control. For fundamentalists, Yuval-Davis proposes, freedom for women spells 'social disaster'.[6] Writing specifically in relation to Islam, Deniz Kandiyoti argues that women in Muslim societies are perceived to be the guardians of Islam and of the nation's boundaries. Hence 'the

compelling association between women's appropriate place and conduct, however defined, and notions of cultural authenticity is a persistent
theme', she says.[7] Nationalism in Muslim societies has been closely associated with movements against Western colonialism and imperialism,
which attempted to secularise and liberate women.[8] According to
Kandiyoti, such discourses of authenticity are smokescreens, deflecting
attention from intractable class, religious and ethnic divisions within
contemporary Muslim societies onto women's attire and conduct.[9] In
this sense Islam has become a populist vehicle of resistance to
'Westernised' elites in these societies.

Deploying ingenious hermeneutical logic to interpret the Koranic verse
on veiling, Fatima Mernissi argues critically that just as the hijab was first
ordained by the Prophet in a year of crisis, so too it has become '... a solution for a pressing crisis. Protecting women from change by veiling them
and shutting them out of the world has echoes of closing the community
to protect it from the West.'[10] Under these circumstances dress comes to
be a symbolically laden vehicle which may stand alternatively for modesty, a defiant, oppositional 'Islam', or a rejection of 'tradition'. This has
been evident in the politics of multiculturalism surrounding veiling,
forced marriages and honour killings among Muslim and South Asian
immigrant groups in contemporary Western Europe. The present chapter
focuses comparatively on discourses in the press and public sphere in
France and Britain in order to illustrate that in both countries, the 'problem' of Muslims who refuse to integrate has emerged as a public debate
about the politics of intimacy and sexual modesty.

The politics of embodiment

The rise of radical Islamic movements in the Muslim world and their
global reach appears to be tangibly signalled by women and young girls
wearing the Muslim headscarf, the hijab. Yet although inspired, perhaps, by the same sort of global Islamic rhetoric that moves the extremists, the hijab wearers are the children of postcolonial migrants, the
majority of whom have no links to these movements. Nevertheless,
some of the problems associated with the integration of an earlier generation of South Asian migrants to Britain have once again surfaced as
their children reach marriageable age in very large numbers. In Britain,
unlike France, these problems are often cast as the product of 'backward' Muslim or Asian 'traditions', rather than the recent rise in Islamic
radicalism. Nevertheless they feed on a perception of Muslims in particular as a problematic minority refusing to integrate.

To consider some of these issues, arising out of the politics of embodiment within Muslim diasporic communities in Europe, they need to be seen as part of a more complex cultural dynamics generated by international migration. In Britain the wearing of Muslim head coverings to school has been treated pragmatically and integrated in most cases into the school uniform, a point to which I return below. While the growing number of girls wearing hijabs still represents a significant movement in Britain, perhaps even a social movement, until quite recently it has not been imbricated in legal issues as in France, nor is it seen as a threat to national identity, as in the French case.[11] In March 2006, however, the case of a young schoolgirl in Britain wishing to wear the *jilbab* (a long black gown and veil) to school was the subject of extensive litigation, and the case was finally only settled in the House of Lords.[12]

Unlike France, Britain appeared on the whole to be distinguished by a virtual absence of conflict over an 'Islamic' school uniform. Then, in October 2006, the public debate on the *niqab* spiralled out of control. This followed a pronouncement by Jack Straw, former Home Secretary, that it signalled 'separation and difference', impeded communication and struck at community relations. Ruth Kelly, the Communities Secretary, questioned whether 'multiculturalism' was 'encouraging segregation'. A young *niqab*-wearing teaching assistant was suspended with ministerial blessing. The secondary symbolic meanings of the veil in its extreme form were implicitly linked to hidden terror, gender violence and extremism. In a riposte in *The Times* the Archibishop of Canterbury, Rowan Williams, defended the right to wear religious symbols, including the *niqab*, on the grounds that the state is 'not the source of morality'.[13] *The Times* front page leader interprets his comments as reflecting 'concern within the Church that some members of the Government want to see Britain follow the same route as France'.[14]

But even before the *niqab* affair, the politics of embodiment concerning the Muslim (and more broadly, South Asian) community in Britain were the subject of public debate in the media and speeches by politicians. These culminated, in 2004, in the setting up of a Forced Marriage Unit, and in 2005, the proposal for a specific law against forced marriages,[15] ultimately rejected in 2006 after a lengthy consultation process. While it was agreed that the law would send out a strong *symbolic* message, most groups consulted (including women, children and ethnic organisations, law societies, the Bar Council, local authorities and the police) felt it would push the practice underground, since girls would be unwilling to testify against their parents. Instead, they recommended a strong educational and training campaign and safety network for young women. This rejection of the law as an instrument of social engineering typifies the contrast between Britain and France. Instead of criminalisation, a stream of conferences has addressed the problem of 'honour' murders. Figures given by *The Times* in 2006 highlight the dimensions of the problem, although researchers admit that accurate statistics are impossible to obtain:

> Between 2003 and 2005, 518 forced marriages were recorded in London, and in 2005 more than 140 in Bradford. Campaigners say those are merely the tip of the iceberg. Most cases in Britain involve Muslim families, although the practice is not restricted to any particular religious or ethnic group. Most victims are aged between 16 and 20 and many suffer physical assault, death threats and false imprisonment, usually at the hands of close family members. Suicide rates among young Asian women are more than three times the national average and about 12 women every year die as a result of so-called 'honour killings'.[16]

Like the customary veil, the politics of marriage are embedded in customary notions of honour and shame, which surround the right to control the sexuality and reproductive powers of young people, particularly younger women's bodies, specifically by men and more generally by an older generation of migrants. The wearing of a head covering signals respect within this honour and shame symbolic complex. It is a sign of sexual modesty, and cannot be understood apart from it. Even if, somewhat contradictorily, the adoption of the scarf by young Muslim girls is conceived of as a *rejection* of tradition, they are unable to escape its self-evident connection (at least for the older generation of immigrants) to traditional ideas about what constitutes *dishonour*.

Honour, shame and the 'deterritorialisation' of female sexual modesty

The adoption by women of a uniform scarf style and global discourse has created an apparent disjunction between a deterritorialised notion of Islamic female modesty and traditional South Asian notions of honour and shame, which are always highly local and contextualised in family and community relations. The deterritorialised scarf is often taken to be merely a 'symbol' of Islamic purity. Yet despite the denial of continuity, both the Islamic scarf and ideas about honour and shame stem from the same stress on female sexual modesty and control within a politics of embodiment.

Broadly speaking, notions of honour and shame are located at the point where familial politics and the politics of religion, tribe and nation meet. Their significance is thus inevitably ambiguous, dynamic and shifting. Indeed, although notions of honour and shame are widely prevalent across feudal and tribal societies in the Mediterranean and Asia, the social context in which the honour and shame symbolic complex is played out can create radical shifts in meaning.[17] This is particularly evident in the case of the Islamic scarf, but also more broadly in the way in which notions of honour and shame are tolerated and respected in different social contexts.

The limits of the 'sexual' honour and shame model

The anthropological honour and shame model, to the extent that it focuses exclusively on female sexual transgression, is arguably limited in several important senses. Above all, violence against women in Punjabi society takes many different forms and is the outcome of a wide range of complex conflicts inside the family and between different family members, affines and kinsmen. Second, 'honour' (*izzat*) is a very broad concept: it refers to caste and class status, to public reputation, and to symbolic capital accumulated through generosity towards guests and inferiors. Since it covers a wide range of issues of which the politics of sexuality and reproduction or alliance is only one, its use for analytic purposes is misleading.

In the migration context in Britain, reputation and honour (*izzat*) among Punjabi immigrants from all the different faith communities, like violence against women, is deeply embedded in the politics of marriage and the (extended) family (*rishtedar, biradari*), but also in the politics of community.[18] This is not simply a question of patriarchal domination but of generational differences. Moreover, as in the Punjab, in Britain too violence against women takes many different forms and is related to complex intra-familial relations, often involving the extended family, parents-in-law, sisters-in-law and other affines. Yet it seems evident that slurs to a family's reputation, a loss of face, as well as fear of violence from family members who feel their 'honour' has been attacked, are important factors for the parental migrant generation when they consider the marriage options open to their sons and daughters. At present the younger generation, whose parents arrived in Britain in the late 1970s, is reaching marriageable age in large numbers, and hence the argument about the pros and cons of arranged marriage both within and beyond the community has intensified considerably.

As the number of violent incidents surrounding the politics of arranged marriages has multiplied, these have become the topic of debate in the press and pronouncements by politicians. The pictures of young girls murdered or kidnapped, and stories of their rescue by boyfriends or the Foreign Office's special unit in Pakistan, regularly make the headlines in Britain, underlining the problematic of immigrants who refuse to integrate, and their backward, repressive and violent attitude to women. In many cases, there is considerable ambiguity about the causes of violence against women. In one murder case of a bride on her wedding day, which occurred in Birmingham, it was unclear whether this was an honour killing or not, and in what sense. The girl was marrying the man of her choice with her father's consent. It appears that a cousin who may have wanted to marry her himself enlisted an older relative to murder her on the day of her wedding.[19]

'Honour' and 'shame' (*ghairat* or *izzat, sharm*) can be rhetorical devices for eliciting obedience from recalcitrant or rebellious children who refuse to marry according to parental choices. Increasingly in Britain arranged marriage is being scrutinised, criticised and modified by a range of officials, parliamentarians and by young people themselves. Although officially children still accede to their parents' marriage arrangements, in practice, as the number of unsuccessful marriages leading to divorce multiplies, the perception is growing that arranged marriages in Britain based on parental choices no longer 'work'. As children become less willing to accept their parents' judgement, conflicts within the family have multiplied and have led, in extreme cases, to publicity in the local and national press. Young people seek alternative ways of finding a match, even using the Internet.[20] Generally speaking, arranged marriages are seen as acceptable, although archaic and somewhat bizarre, by the British public, but there is broad consensus that young people should not be forced into marriage against their will. As British citizens they have the right to choose whom and when they want to marry. Yet the line between arranged and forced marriages is a fine one, as young people do not wish to cause their parents distress.[21]

Hence, the public debate in Britain has focused on 'forced marriages'. In some of these, girls are taken to the Punjab, apparently on holiday, and then forced to marry relatives. They are essentially abducted and kept locked up in some remote village. In many cases, psychological pressure is exerted on young men as well as women to agree to marriages. A report for the Foreign and Commonwealth Office commissioned in 2002 found that parents see marriage as a solution to the 'problem' of sons and daughters whom they feel are out of control: some may have boyfriends or girlfriends, some may be taking drugs or involved in petty crime.[22] Yet marriage may simply multiply such problems.

The transnational connection

After lengthy procrastination,[23] the Foreign and Commonwealth Office has set up a special Community Liaison Unit in Pakistan to detect and rescue kidnapped brides. According to *The Guardian*, the Unit helped repatriate 75 young British people sent abroad for marriage between 2000 and 2002 and dealt with 440 cases over that same period. In 2003 the Unit dealt with 250 cases, including 50 emergency repatriations.[24] In 2002, a 22-year-old Pakistani woman, Narina Anwar, was awarded a CBE for campaigning against forced marriages, having been subjected to one herself and subsequently ostracised by her family when she escaped. In Pakistan a court annulled the marriage of a young English Pakistani woman forced into marriage in a landmark case in which she gave evidence to the high court in Islamabad.[25] There are said to be between 1000 and 2000 forced marriages a year occurring in the UK.

Pakistani marriage in Britain

Despite the tensions surrounding arranged marriages, most researchers have found continued high rates of intercontinental and intra-caste marriages (over 50 per cent) between British Pakistani spouses and brides or grooms in Pakistan.[26] Transnational marriages renew connections with absent kin and express the diasporic yearning of migrants. But pressure is also apparently exerted by close relatives in Pakistan who use marriage as a route for their children to migrate legally to Britain. Despite their hopes, recent research has shown, however, that in-marrying spouses often suffer isolation, and have poor employment prospects.[27] Most Pakistani children are compliant and agree, however reluctantly, to cousin and intercontinental marriages.[28] Home Office statistics showed an influx of 15,000 prospective marriage partners (male and female) from the Indian subcontinent arriving in Britain in 2001 alone, the vast majority arranged by parents for their British-born children. Charsley reports that in 2000, there were 10,000 in-marrying spouses, both men and women, from Pakistan. Islam permits marriage with a wide range of close kin and affines, and it seems that the majority of Pakistani marriages continue to take place within the *biradari*, a local agnatic lineage and, more widely, an ego-focused kindred of traceable affines and consanguineous kin. The notion of *biradari* mediates between kinship, locality and *zat* (caste) and *biradaris* are ranked and reflect class and caste status.

Under the circumstances in which there are real intergenerational differences or cultural disparities between spouses, physical and psychological violence against women is widely reported. In Britain there are South Asian women's refuges which have been set up in different parts of the country. Young girls and battered wives go into hiding. Women's campaign groups advocate for the rights of Asian women suffering from violence in the home. Among these, Southall Black Sisters is the oldest and best known organisation.[29] The media and press report on 'bounty hunters' sent to recover escaped daughters or wives.

A critique of this type of reporting, and of pronouncements against intercontinental and forced marriages by politicians such as David Blunkett, the Home Secretary in 2002, and Ann Cryer, MP for Bradford South, has come not only from community leaders denying the extent of the problem, but from some South Asian women scholars. Hence, Farzana Shain has criticised the emergence of a racialised discourse of 'cultural pathology'. This implies (she says) that 'something is inherently inferior in the familial and cultural background of [minorities]'.[30] Yet according to Siddiqui, a meeting organised by Southall Black Sisters between the Home Office Working Group and survivors of forced marriage was 'highly emotional...The women made clear that community leaders did not speak for them.'[31] Ultimately, Siddiqui resigned from the Home Office Working Group over the issue of mediation, which the organisation rejected. Clearly, however, the public and media debate in Britain surrounding forced marriages and 'honour' killings is fraught with the risk of further stigmatising a vulnerable minority in crisis. As Siddiqui says: 'There is a clear and present danger of issues like forced marriage being hijacked by racists, which is why we insist on mainstreaming it in the debate on domestic violence. We find ourselves standing once again on the slippery intersection between race and gender.'[32]

Nevertheless, problems surrounding so-called honour killings, forced marriages, under-age 'community' marriages and the like, along with riots in northern British cities in the summer of 2001, have led to repeated calls by British politicians for Asians or Muslims to 'integrate' into the community. Following David Blunkett, Peter Hain, the Europe Minister in 2002, accused the Muslim community of being 'isolationist' and posing a major threat to harmony in Britain.[33] Invocations of this type by British politicians have been a familiar response since the Rushdie affair, but until recently there was no attempt to legislate in order to force so-called integration. Following the 7 July 2005 London bombings, however, the controversial Terrorism Act 2006 introduced a new offence of the 'glorification' of terror, indicating a policy shift. In the past, politicians repeatedly used their position to stress the peaceful and tolerant nature of the 'true' Islam and the contribution minorities have made to multicultural Britain. Persuasive rhetoric rather than the law has been the chosen British way of dealing with minorities perceived to be problematic, whether religious or ethnic. The French use of the law as a *symbolic* tool has never been favoured in Britain, and the French legal banning of religious symbols in schools, clearly targeting the Muslim scarf, has occasioned astonishment, ridicule and derision in Britain. This points to the very different context in which religious minorities have been integrated as citizens into British society.

It is evident from the Scottish CPB(S) report that despite the apparent success of some arranged marriages, the extreme violence against women reported in the media appears to be only the tip of the iceberg. Even middle-class urban families who arrange marriages *in Britain* for their daughters with non-related, apparently middle-class families, may encounter severe and unanticipated problems with sons-in-law. As for the children themselves, they are increasingly beginning to find their own marriage partners first, before marriages are arranged by parents post hoc. These are called 'love' marriages. A recent report on Bangladeshi women in the East End quotes many of the older generation of women as saying they would not like to force their children into an unwanted marriage in case the marriage breaks down.[34] But despite such statements, there is little evidence that parents have stopped actively intervening in their children's marriage choices.

Strategic veiling

One strategy used by young Muslims in Britain to contend with these conflicts is to adopt voluntarily what seems on the surface to be an extremist Islamic ideology of veiling and purdah for women, beards and prayer for men. Being observant Muslims empowers these young men and women with the right to choose their own marriage partners, even against the will of their parents. They accuse their parents of being ignorant, locked into false or mistaken parochial 'customs' and 'traditions' of the old country, which, according to the girls, distort 'true' Islam.[35] As Dwyer was told, 'They (the parents) mix up religion and culture.'[36] The girls argue that Islam accords equality to men and women, that it requires young people's consent to a marriage and allows them to choose their own partner, and even to associate with their fiancés before marriage. Islam also opens up a much wider marriage market for young people. At the same time upper-middle-class Pakistanis often refuse marriages for their sons with veiled girls, which indicates that wearing the hijab is still often associated for elite Punjabis with lower-middle-class status.

Like sexual norms surrounding marriage, the *dupatta* is embedded in and embodies the female code of honour in subtle and nuanced ways. But is the same true of the hijab? Writing about dress among South Asians in Britain, Claire Dwyer argues that it is 'a powerful and overde-termined marker of difference', an essentialised symbol of a 'traditional' identity associated with being South Asian or Muslim.[37] Such essential-ist definitions are imposed by teachers and pupils, whether or not young schoolgirls themselves want to embrace them. By contrast, European clothes are regarded as modern, secular and hence progressive. Signifi-cantly, according to Dwyer, in the UK the wearing of headscarves is understood as an expression not of religion but of 'ethnic identity', and as such it is protected by law for women of South Asian origin. Despite its association with tradition, however, like in the rest of the Muslim world, the hijab in Britain expresses a 'new' identity, part of a deterrito-rialised global movement. That identity is not necessarily, however, 'fundamentalist', 'Islamist' or radical, since its meaning and the politics of embodiment it represents may differ widely in different contexts and even individually.

Two confrontations surrounding veiling occurred in Britain. The first, in 1989, in a middle-class grammar school, was settled in favour of two sisters who challenged the school to allow them to wear the head-scarf.[38] In the second, a girl who was excluded from school for wearing the *jilbab,* a head-to-toe covering, initially won her case on appeal but this was overturned by the House of Lords.

The case of the two Alwi sisters who won the right to wear scarfs to Altrincham grammar school, against the conventions of the school uni-form, highlights the fact that young Pakistani girls in Britain can choose from a range of 'identities', and position themselves through clothing and lifestyle closer to their ethnic, strictly religious or Western secular poles.[39] Wearing the hijab asserts identification broadly with the Middle East, the heartland of Islam and Arabic, the sacred language of the Koran, and thus with Islam as a universal religion, beyond South Asia. In this sense wearing the hijab is not particularly radical, although some young Muslim associations do deploy a radical, anti-Western rhet-oric. Haleh Afshar has argued that the headscarf confers dignity and makes the girls 'part of the great anti-imperialist Islamic movement'.[40]

The hijab raises a series of questions about meaning, diasporic mobil-isation, identity, multiculturalism, cultural difference, political Islam, gender, agency, transnationalism and globalisation. A uniformity of appearance (a scarf) disguises the fact that the meanings of veiling are themselves veiled (and different). Indeed, as Clifford Geertz suggests,[41] the political dimensions of Muslim veiling should not blind us to the quest for personal meaning that also motivates this process.

Meanings vary according to context. In the debating and passing of the law, the French have stressed the pernicious features of veiling, associated in the public imagination with violently forced veiling in Islamist countries such as Iran after the revolution and Afghanistan under the Taliban: the exploitation and subordination of women, their exclusion from education, public office and the professions. This existential degradation of women's autonomy and freedom is highlighted by Azar Nafisi in her book, *Reading Lolita in Tehran*,[42] in which she describes the agonising sense of oppression and loss of agency which forced veiling has created for Westernised women intellectuals and the middle classes in Iran. Drawing on such extreme cases, the French see the headscarf as a straightforward sign of female oppression and the totalitarian, anti-emancipatory tendencies of Islamist groups, which also espouse terror against Western targets. They define veiling as primarily *religious,* and associate it with extremist terror groups, such as al-Qaida.

Schools as pure spaces

This French position needs to be set in the context of a specific philosophical approach to education for citizenship. Educational theorists, according to Elaine Unterhalter, are divided on the role that education should play in the making of citizens as equal but different.[43] French education, following Kant, starts from the notion of 'abstract universality',[44] of individual subjects stripped of any divisive collective identities and affiliations. These are relegated to the private sphere. Hence French schools are conceived of as pure spaces in which subjects are free to develop their personal subjectivity, unencumbered by collective, especially religious, differences. This relates, of course, also to the historical struggle against the educational hegemony of the Catholic Church in France. By contrast, multicultural and multi-faith education in Britain, rather than regarding schools as spaces set apart from society, sees schools as spaces in which the private and public ambiguously meet. English schools are thus conceived of as arenas in which differences ought to be taught and discussed openly from a position of neutrality, in order to educate subjects towards mutual tolerance and respect for difference.

Although the hijab has pernicious associations for women in some Muslim countries, its association with religiosity is at best ambiguous since it is, above all, an embodied guarantor of personal modesty. Yet in France, girls who wear the headscarf are seen as the vanguard of a potential and dangerous French Muslim attack on the secular institutions of the state. The scarf is grasped as the precursor of further and more extreme demands for separate institutions and special treatment, and for the predatory expansion and colonisation of public spaces. The French Commission that recommended a law against veiling, was told by unveiled Muslim girls that they had been subjected to unacceptable pressure to veil from peers or the community at large.

In a secular context in which religion is relegated to civil society and the private sphere, veiling may take on non-extremist meanings, and its toleration in public spaces may become a crucible of multicultural tolerance. Hence, while it is still possible to regard veiling as a public political issue, it also has subjective meanings for the girls who wear a headscarf. Certainly in Britain, by asserting their command of the 'true' Islam, signalled by their wearing of the hijab, girls are claiming that Islam accords equal rights to men and women, and are thus opening up for themselves spaces for autonomous decision-making. This includes, above all, the right to choose their own marriage partners, but also, perhaps equally importantly, the right to work, to be educated, to go to university, to move around in public unchaperoned, and much else besides. It also resolves the ambiguities of being young, British and Muslim, by signalling that some activities, such as drinking or clubbing, are out of bounds. Veiling is a mobile form of purdah that secludes a woman while at the same time allowing her to move around freely in public. For Pakistani girls living in encapsulated, highly conservative, immigrant residential areas, veiling is often a small price to pay for freedom of movement.

It is possible that some girls are forced to wear the scarf against their will. Seen sociologically, much depends on where the girls are coming from: their ethnic or class background, the kind of neighbourhood in which they live, family class mobility or assimilation, parental secular, religious or political commitments. But equally, by wearing the hijab women students are signalling to Muslim male students that they are not available sexually to non-Muslims, and at the same time obliquely demanding that the men too behave morally and avoid playing around with non-Muslim girls. Away from their parents, these students create their own society in which they can mix freely under the mantle of Islam. Islam thus becomes the guarantor of moral behaviour in mixed social gatherings in which an approved marriage market is created away from parental supervision.

Because veiling is a protective shield against the male gaze, it is useful in preventing unwanted advances by young men, especially for girls who live in densely crowded immigrant neighbourhoods or who study in mixed schools or at university. Muslim women often find English 'clubbing' culture unpalatable, with its heavy drinking of alcohol and sexual promiscuity. Veiling thus legitimises their avoidance of such embarrassing contexts. It similarly provides protection in rough neighbourhoods where women may be vulnerable to violence. A veiled woman is signalling that she is not to be touched. In this respects it conforms with the honour and shame code of conduct and demands respect from outsiders.[45]

Much depends on the meaning of the hijab. If it is merely a higher-order 'symbol' of Islam, worn as a form of political protest, then unveiling does not imply a sense of shame, and the veil is not part of the politics of embodiment. It can easily be removed. If, however, veiling is a sign not merely of religion but of *modesty* (women are not obliged to veil at home or in front of other women; they only veil religiously when praying, as a sign of respect), this is surely where the *human rights* debate lies, given that the headscarf causes no harm, either to the wearer or the spectator. If veiling as practised by women in secular democracies expresses their personal will, identity and subjectivity, and if it is associated with a sense of embodied integrity, modesty and piety, then a legal prohibition of it becomes highly problematic. The idea that an essentially political (and not religious) battle can be fought over the bodies of powerless young girls would seem to be a basic infringement of human rights. As Moruzzi argues,[46] young Muslims in France are being 'forced to deal with a doubly constructed gender identity that [they] are not allowed to negotiate', that of the state and that of being a marginalised immigrant minority. Similarly, Seyla Benhabib, who, like others, highlights the resignification of veiled meanings, recommends that young teenagers be asked to 'account for themselves and their doings at least to their school communities', rather than the state 'dictating' the meanings of their actions before 'penalising and criminalizing' them.[47]

In Britain, unlike France, religion is taught in schools. Indeed, in Britain there are no purely secular state schools, since all state schools have religious assembly at least three times a week, and all schools teach religious studies as part of the national curriculum (recently, other religious groups have been allowed to convene their own assemblies). This usually includes basic instruction in Christianity, Judaism, Islam, Hinduism and Buddhism. The pedagogical argument is that this relativises all religions. All state schools celebrate Christmas with nativity plays, while schools in immigrant neighbourhoods usually celebrate Muslim, Sikh and Hindu festivals as well, depending on the composition of the school.[48] At the same time it has been argued that despite invocations of secularity, French schooling is implicitly Christian, while most French public holidays are saints' days.[49] In Britain, although Anglicanism is the established religion, other religious dignitaries are also accorded public respect, while most public holidays, apart from Christmas and Good Friday, are 'bank' holidays. The French defend the decision to prohibit veiling in secular schools on the grounds that they fund religious schools. These too, however, are regarded as 'pure' (and hence ghettoised) spaces, but in any case, at the time the law was passed there were no state-funded Muslim schools in France.

Accommodation of ethnic minorities has been negotiated piecemeal in Britain, almost entirely at local authority level, with little fanfare or public crisis. Over time, for example, Muslims have been granted halal meals for Muslim schoolchildren, Muslim cemeteries, mosque building sites and urban planning permission, spaces for prayer in universities and airports, voluntary-aided Muslim state schools (after quite a long struggle), and the right to wear trousers and the headscarf in school, as long as the trousers and headscarf conform to the school uniform.

The question is, of course, to what extent are girls in Britain or France (and their parents) being pressured into adopting the headscarf in response to violent threats from Islamic extremists? Moral pressure is inevitable in close-knit communities. But even if this is so, from an English perspective such pressures are perhaps best tackled through public debate and education within schools. A law is a very blunt tool and its consequences are likely to be counterproductive. It may produce a school boycott and exclusions from school. It leads to a *Kulturkampf,* a cultural clash, and is likely thus to generate a Muslim backlash and a general sense of alienation and rejection, even among those Muslims who do not veil. During the year leading up to the French law's implementation, diasporic Muslims throughout Europe, and not just France, began gearing up for public protest, holding demonstrations in France, Belgium, Copenhagen and London.[50] The Mayor of London, Ken Livingstone, hosted a conference held by the Assembly for the Protection of Hijab (or 'pro-Hijab') on 12 July 2004. An International Hijab Solidarity Day was set for 4 September 2004, the day the French school year began. But when this date finally arrived, there were no demonstrations and the vast majority of schoolgirls complied with the law, removed their hijabs, encouraged also by French Muslim official representatives and their parents, the latter quoted as saying that the girls' education came first.[51]

The virtual collapse of the protest raises questions about the meaning of the hijab for girls and their parents. Was it merely an exterior symbol of faith and 'cultural defiance', to be discarded at ease? Nevertheless, resort to the law in France, and possibly in Germany, Belgium and the Netherlands, reveals a clear divide between French and Anglo-American legal cultures. On 29 June 2004, the European Court of Human Rights upheld a Turkish prohibition on student veiling at university. Against that, members of the UN Committee on the Rights of the Child sharply criticised the French law. Rather than Huntington's clash of civilisations between Islam and Christianity, the civilisational clash appears to be between political cultures that tolerate visible pluralism and those that do not. Although the French cite the historical tradition of secularism and the turn-of-twentieth-century battle against the Catholic Church to secure secular education as justifications for the law, this ignores the significance of subsequent historical events in Europe. The historical invocation of secularism needs to be set against a historical record of racist intolerance against assimilated, invisible minorities such as the Jews, which is still only partly acknowledged by the French and perhaps the German state. The historical legitimation for *laïcité* and, more broadly, for the universalist egalitarian principles of the French Revolution, rings extremely hollow pitched against that more recent record where public invisibility did not safeguard Jewish lives. The fact that no lessons appear to have been learnt from this shameful past points to a wider tendency towards selective historical amnesia in the construction of national histories. [52]

Muslims have argued that the law in France is racist since it is really intended to target them specifically and attack their religion and culture under the false banner of secularism. Young French women claim that the hijab is 'part of my identity' and argue that they should be able to show 'who and what we are'.[53] There does appear to be some truth in this claim. One also senses from remarks by French politicians that young girls' veiling represents a deep threat to French cultural notions of sexual liberation, which in practice favour male sexual licence, although the rhetoric is cast in terms of the sexual freedoms gained in France against the Catholic Church. Sexual freedom, like secularism itself, is here elevated to sacred status, as Foucault has argued. Indeed, Joan Wallach Scott argues, perhaps 'the most stunning contradiction' in the passing of the law which she sees as 'a form of deep denial', a 'gesture of impotence', 'was the alliance of so many French feminists, who, in the name of the emancipation of Muslim girls, rushed to support a law that offered the status quo in France (women as the *object* of male desire!) as a universal model of women's liberation'.[54]

Conclusion

Multiculturalists argue that educating citizens to tolerate overt public signs of difference is crucial to living together in a plural society. The banner of secularism or abstract universalism may have been appropriate to an earlier phase of nationalism. The Second World War proved, however, that cultural assimilation does not necessarily lead to the erasure of difference. Both in Iran after the revolution and in Nazi Germany, highly assimilated minorities were forced to bear the stigmata of their exclusion. Given this history, the right of minorities to advertise their differences publicly would seem to be a basic right especially when, as in the case of the scarf, the practice causes no harm to others.

At the same time, the honour and shame symbolic complex, which in Muslim societies includes veiling as a sign of modesty, clearly does have its pernicious side for the Muslims of Britain, expressed in violence against young girls in particular. There is much that can be debated in schools about the right of children to make independent moral decisions, to own their own bodies, to choose their own partners. It is ironic, to my mind, that the law has been applied to schools, which are the very places where citizens may be educated and where debates about clothing, beliefs and values can take place unimpeded.

Multicultural education in Britain is perhaps a beacon of tolerance in an otherwise bleak picture. Since their migration Muslims in Britain have in other respects been locked in repeated confrontation with the state.[55] The present chapter has argued that despite the pragmatic accommodation of Muslim religiosity in Britain, the media and politicians continue to represent South Asian immigrants, including Muslims, in the public sphere as 'problems'. For a liberal society what seems most worrying is the politics of sexuality and embodiment, of honour and shame, that apparently continue to prevail among some sections of the migrant generation (and sometimes among their sons), evident in the way that South Asian Muslim, Sikh or Hindu parents continue to attempt to retain control of their children's sexual and reproductive behaviour and choices, and to punish them violently if they transgress and are felt to compromise family 'honour'. As I also argue, however, the law on its own cannot possibly control familial violence, just as it cannot prohibit the growing ambivalence in children's attitudes to parental authority, or an emergent consciousness empowering young women.

This chapter has highlighted processes of higher-order, deterritorialised symbolisation that invoke new types of authority and appeal to different principles and constituencies. These lead to apparently contradictory messages as in the case of the hijab, which may be used by young Muslim girls as a symbol of independence and the right to claim autonomous agency vis-à-vis their parents, while at the same time the girls also signal their defiance of the wider society perceived to be hostile to Islam. In a sense, then, it might be argued that the adoption of a 'new' Islamic identity signalled by the veil/scarf is a cunning solution invented by young people themselves to *appear* to honour their parents (and to defy others in positions of authority) while nevertheless demanding the right to decide their own destiny.

Notes

1. A version of this chapter was first presented to a conference on Honour and Shame in Europe, at the University of Western Australia in July 2003. Later versions were presented at Ben Gurion University of the Negev, the International Sociological Association Conference on 'Racisms, Sexisms and Contemporary Politics of Belonging/s' in August 2004, London, and at a conference on 'The Constructions of Minority Identities in Britain and France' in Bristol University in September 2004. I wish to thank all the various participants at these conferences for their incisive comments.
2. M. Foucault, *The History of Sexuality*, Vol. I: *An Introduction* (New York: Vintage Books, 1980).
3. Ibid., pp. 7–8.
4. C. Pateman, *The Social Contract* (Cambridge: Polity Press, 1988).
5. P. Werbner, *Pilgrims of Love: the Anthropology of a Global Sufi Cult* (London: Hurst Publishers, 2003).
6. N. Yuval-Davis, 'Fundamentalism, Multiculturalism and Women in Britain,' in J. Donald and A. Rattansi (eds), *'Race', Culture and Difference* (London: Sage Publications, 1992), p. 285.
7. D. Kandiyoti, *Women, Islam and the State* (London: Macmillan, 1991), p. 7.
8. L. Ahmed, *Women and Gender in Islam* (New Haven: Yale University Press, 1992), p. 130.
9. Kandiyoti, *Women, Islam and the State*, p. 8.
10. F. Mernissi, *Women and Islam: an Historical and Theological Enquiry* (Oxford: Basil Blackwell, 1991), p. 99.
11. See N. Moruzzi, 'A Problem with Headscarves: Contemporary Complexities of Political and Social Identity', *Political Theory*, 22/4 (1994), pp. 633–79, for an insightful analysis of the 1989 and recent French scarf affairs, the responses and events leading to them.

12. The Court of Appeal found Denbigh High School had denied Shabina Begum the right to manifest her religion in refusing to allow her to wear a *jilbab* but in a unanimous ruling, judges at the House of Lords overturned that, saying that the Luton school had 'taken immense pains to devise a uniform policy which respected Muslim beliefs', and that it had done so 'in an inclusive, unthreatening and uncompetitive way'. The Law Lords added that 'The rules laid down were as far from being mindless as uniform rules could ever be. It appeared the rules were acceptable to mainstream Muslim opinion.' Shabina Begum had chosen a school which 'went to unusual lengths to inform parents of its uniform policy', and there was no interference with her right to manifest her religion as she had chosen a school where such a policy existed (BBC News online, 22 March 2006).
13. *The Times*, 27 October 2006.
14. R. Gledhill, 'Let People Wear Cross or Veil, Says Archibishop', *The Times*, ibid.
15. Foreign and Commonwealth Office and Home Office, *Forced Marriage: a Wrong not a Right* (London: HMSO, 2005).
16. Forced marriage is defined by the Foreign and Commonwealth Office as 'a marriage conducted without the full and free consent of both parties, where duress is a factor'. According to *The Times*,

    Of 518 'forced marriage-related incidents' reported in London between 2003 and 2005, 135 involved threats to kill, 114 assault and 65 false imprisonment. Cases generally involve women aged between 15 and 24. One in four victims is under the age of 18. One in 17 victims is male. Although 80 per cent of those responsible for coercing people into forced marriage are male, one in five is female. The vast majority are members of the same family as the victim. Of 109 so-called 'honour killings' studied by the Homicide Prevention Unit, one in five was linked to forced marriage.

    The paper reports that a Crown Prosecution director of Muslim origin said that 'while more than 60 per cent of cases involve Muslim families, particularly Pakistani Muslim families, there is no faith foundation for it. A forced marriage in Islam is no marriage at all' (A. Norfolk, 'Despair as Forced Marriages Stay Legal', *The Times*, 24 July 2006).
17. It is beyond the scope of this chapter to discuss the debate on honour and shame in the Mediterranean, but there too the stress has been on nuance, positioning and interpretation. See R.J. Coombe, 'Barren Ground: Re-conceiving Honour and Shame in the Field of Mediterranean Ethnography', *Anthropologica*, XXXII (1990), pp. 221–31.
18. On this see P. Werbner, *Imagined Diasporas among Manchester Muslims* (Oxford: James Currey, 2002).
19. J. Vasagar, 'Freedom to Choose may have Cost Bride her Life', *The Guardian*, 18 January 2003.
20. A. Khan, 'How to Net a Husband', *The Guardian G2*, 19 May 2003.
21. H. Siddiqui, '"It was Written in her Kismet": Forced Marriage', in R. Gupta (ed.), *From Homebreakers to Jailbreakers: Southall Black Sisters* (London: Zed Books, 2003), p. 70.
22. Y. Samad and J. Eade, *Foreign and Commonwealth Office Report on Community Perceptions of Forced Marriage* (London: HMSO, 2002).

23. According to Siddiqui this was due in part to the ambiguity arising from dual (Pakistani and British) citizenship, even for young people born in Britain, and partly to what Southall Black Sisters regard as misguided multicultural policy of non-interference. Siddiqui, '"It was Written in her Kismet": Forced Marriage', p. 72.

24. CBPS, *Incompatible Marriage Project (IMP)* (Edinburgh: Council of British Pakistanis Scotland, 2004), p. 14.

25. Z. Abbas and J. Wilson, 'British Woman in Forced Marriage Freed', *The Guardian*, 8 May 2003.

26. K. Charsley, 'Unhappy Husbands: Masculinity and Migration in Transnational Pakistani Marriages', *JRAI*, 11 (2005), pp. 185–6.

27. Ibid.

28. J. Jacobson, *Islam in Transition: Religion and Identity among British Pakistani Youth* (London: Routledge, 1998).

29. For a detailed account of Southall Black Sisters' campaign against forced marriages and other honour crimes see Siddiqui, '"It was Written in her Kismet": Forced Marriage', who presents detailed accounts of some tragic cases. Tarlo reflects on the difficulties of anthropological research and writing about a women's Islamic movement, Hizb ut-Tahrir, protesting against the hijab ban in France. See also E. Tarlo, 'Reconsidering Stereotypes: Anthropological Reflections on the Jilbab Controversy', *Anthropology Today*, 21/6 (2005), pp. 13–17.

30. F. Shain, *The Schooling and Identity of Asian Girls* (Stoke-on-Trent: Trentham, 2000), p. 2.

31. Siddiqui, '"It was Written in her Kismet": Forced Marriage', p. 78.

32. Ibid., p. 91.

33. A. Taher, 'Hain Angers "Isolationist" UK Muslims', *Eastern Eye*, 17 May 2002.

34. C. Phillipson et al., *Women in Transition: a Study of the Experiences of Bangladeshi Women Living in Tower Hamlets* (Bristol: the Policy Press, 2003).

35. W. Lyon, 'Islam and Islamic Women in Britain', *Women: a Cultural Review*, 6/1 (1995), pp. 46–56.

36. C. Dwyer, 'Veiled Meanings: Young British Muslim Women and the Negotiation of Difference', *Gender, Place and Culture*, 6/1 (1999), pp. 5–26, p. 17.

37. Ibid., p. 5.

38. On this case in detail see my account in P. Werbner, 'Honour, Shame and the Politics of Sexual Embodiment among South Asian Muslims in Britain and Beyond: an Analysis of Debates in the Public Sphere', *Hagar*, 6/1 (2005), pp. 25–48.

39. See K. Knott and S. Khokher, 'Religious and Ethnic Identity among Young Muslim Women in Bradford', *New Community*, 19/4 (1993), pp. 593–610.

40. H. Afshar, 'Muslim Women in West Yorkshire: Growing up with Real and Imaginary Values amidst Conflicting Views of Self and Society', in H. Afshar and M. Maynard (eds), *The Dynamics of Race and Gender* (London: Taylor and Francis, 1994), p. 143.

41. C. Geertz, *Available Light* (Princeton: Princeton University Press, 2000).

42. A. Nafisi, *Reading Lolita in Tehran* (New York: Random House, 2004).

43. E. Unterhalter, 'Citizenship, Difference and Education: Reflections Inspired by the South African Transition' in N. Yuval-Davis and P. Werbner

(eds), *Women, Citizenship and Difference* (London: Zed Books, 1997), pp. 100–17.

44. S. Amir-Moazami, 'Hybridity and Anti-hybridity: the Islamic Headscarf and its Opponents in the French Public Sphere', in A. Salvatore (ed.), *Muslim Traditions and Modern Techniques of Power*, Yearbook of the Sociology of Islam 3 (Munster: LIT Verlag, 2001), p. 310.

45. See W. Shadid and P.S. van Koningsveld, 'Muslim Dress in Europe: Debates on the Headscarf', *Journal of Islamic Studies*, 16/1 (2005), pp. 35–61.

46. Moruzzi, 'A Problem with Headscarves: Contemporary Complexities of Political and Social Identity', p. 663.

47. S. Benhabib, *The Rights of Others: Aliens, Residents and Citizens* (Cambridge: Cambridge University Press, 2004), pp. 190–1.

48. M. Gillespie, *Television, Ethnicity and Cultural Change* (London: Routledge, 1995).

49. E. Sciolino, 'France has a State Religion: Secularism', *New York Times*, 8 February 2004.

50. On the latter, see Tarlo, 'Reconsidering Stereotypes: Anthropological Reflections on the *Jilbab* Controversy'.

51. This followed the kidnapping of two French journalists in Iraq, with the kidnappers demanding that the French law be repealed. In the face of this violence French Muslims united in solidarity behind the French government.

52. See R. Werbner, 'Introduction: Beyond Oblivion – Confronting Memory Crisis', in R. Werbner (ed.), *Memory and the Postcolony* (London: Zed Books, 1998), pp. 1–20.

53. J. Henley, *The Guardian*, 4 February 2004.

54. J. W. Scott, 'Symptomatic Politics: the Banning of Islamic Head Scarves in French Public Schools', *French Politics, Culture & Society*, 23/3 (2005), pp. 106–27, p. 123.

55. P. Werbner, 'Theorising Complex Diasporas: Purity and Hybridity in the South Asian Public Sphere in Britain', *Journal of Ethnic and Migration Studies*, 30/5 (2004), pp. 895–911.

Select bibliography

Aase, T., *Tournaments of Power: Honor and Revenge in the Contemporary World* (Aldershot: Ashgate, 2002).

Afshar, H. and M. Maynard, M. (eds), *The Dynamics of Race and Gender* (London: Taylor and Francis, 1994).

Ahmed, L., *Women and Gender in Islam* (New Haven: Yale University Press, 1992).

Barker, D.L. and Allen, S. (eds), *Dependence and Exploitation in Work and Marriage* (London: Longman, 1976).

Basit, T. N., *Eastern Values, Western Milieu: Identities and Aspirations of Adolescent British Muslim Girls* (Aldershot: Ashgate, 1997).

Benhabib, S., *The Rights of Others: Aliens, Residents and Citizens* (Cambridge: Cambridge University Press, 2004).

Bourdieu, P., *Sociology in Question* (London: Sage Publications, 1991).

Brah, A., *Cartographies of Diaspora* (London: Routledge, 1996).

CBPS, *Incompatible Marriage Project (IMP)* (Edinburgh: Council of British Pakistanis Scotland, 2004).

Donald, J. and Rattansi, A. (eds), *'Race', Culture and Difference* (London: Sage Publications, 1992).

Foreign and Commonwealth Office and Home Office, *Forced Marriage: a Wrong not a Right* (London: HMSO, 2006).

Foreign and Commonwealth Office, Scottish Executive and Home Office, *Forced Marriage: a Wrong not a Right: Summary of Responses to the Consultation on the Criminalisation of Forced Marriage* (London, HMSO, 2006).

Foucault, M., *The History of Sexuality,* Vol. I: *An Introduction* (New York: Vintage Books, 1980).

Geertz, C., *Available Light* (Princeton: Princeton University Press, 2000).

Gellner, E., *Postmodernism, Reason and Religion* (London: Routledge, 1992).

Gillespie, M., *Television, Ethnicity and Cultural Change* (London: Routledge, 1995).

Göle, N., *The Forbidden Modern* (Ann Arbor: the University of Michigan Press, 1996).

Gupta, R. (ed.), *From Homebreakers to Jailbreakers: Southall Black Sisters* (London: Zed Books, 2003).

Jacobson, J., *Islam in Transition: Religion and Identity among British Pakistani Youth* (London: Routledge, 1998).

Kandiyoti, D., *Women, Islam and the State* (Basingstoke: Macmillan, 1991).

Mernissi, F., *Women and Islam: an Historical and Theological Enquiry* (Oxford: Basil Blackwell, 1991).

Nafisi, A., *Reading Lolita in Tehran* (New York: Random House, 2004).

Pateman, C., *The Social Contract* (Cambridge: Polity Press, 1988).

Phillipson, C., Ahmed, N. and Latimer, J., *Women in Transition: a Study of the Experiences of Bangladeshi Women Living in Tower Hamlets* (Bristol: the Policy Press, 2003).

Salvatore, A. (ed.), *Muslim Traditions and Modern Techniques of Power*, Yearbook of the Sociology of Islam 3 (Munster: LIT Verlag, 2001).

Samad, Y. and Eade, J., Foreign and Commonwealth Office Report on *Community Perceptions of Forced Marriage* (London: HMSO, 2002).

Scott, J. W., *Only Paradoxes to Offer: French Feminists and the Rights of Man* (Cambridge, Mass.: Harvard University Press, 1996).

—— *Parité! Sexual Equality and the Crisis of French Universalism* (Chicago: University of Chicago Press, 2005).

Shain, F., *The Schooling and Identity of Asian Girls* (Stoke-on-Trent: Trentham, 2000).

Shaw, A., *Kinship and Continuity* (London: Routledge, 2000).

Werbner, P., *The Migration Process: Capital, Gifts and Offerings among British Pakistanis* (Oxford: Berg, 2002).

—— *Imagined Diasporas among Manchester Muslims* (Oxford: James Currey, 2002).

—— *Pilgrims of Love: the Anthropology of a Global Sufi Cult* (London: Hurst Publishers, 2003).

Werbner, R. (ed.), *Memory and the Postcolony* (London: Zed Books, 1998).

Yuval-Davis, N. and Werbner, P. (eds), *Women, Citizenship and Difference* (London: Zed Books, 1997).

8
The Construction of Identity, Integration and Participation of Caribbeans in British Society

Harry Goulbourne

Introduction

The aim of this chapter is to contribute to a conversation about the integration of new minority racial and ethnic communities in two major nation states within the European Union: Britain and France. This conversation has gone on for the better part of three decades, but particularly over the last two, and is likely to go on for at least another three decades. And while some commentators thought there were clear signs about possible directions in which these new communities in the two countries were likely to go in the future, this confidence is less certain today. This uncertainty is due to several international and national acts of terrorism from wanton killings in Nairobi and Dar es Salaam in the late 1990s, followed by the outrageous destructions and further killings on 11 September 2001 in New York and Washington, and later similar crimes in Bali and Madrid. The terrorists who perpetrated these crimes sought to justify their action by reference to Islam, and thereby raised new and pressing issues of an international nature but which also urgently require national attention and solutions. In Britain this message was deeply reinforced by the terrorist bombings on the London transport system in July 2005 by young men with British citizenship, claiming to act in the name of Islam, and establishing a climate of fear in all communities, including Muslim communities. These have awoken many to the kinds of enemies there are to what Karl Popper called 'the open society'.

While these developments contextualise international and national debates about the integration of new minorities into majority established populations and societies, my concern here is not with this larger picture of our present national situation of insecurity and uncertainty. Rather, this chapter addresses the relatively small aspect of the integration of people of Caribbean backgrounds into British society over the last half-century, which now appears to be receding in the face of the return of religion as the basis of rights, citizenship and individual action. I hope my comments will be taken as a set of hypotheses which are not empirically verified here, and that they are taken in the spirit of an invitation for, and not a closure on, discussion in what is a dynamic and changing situation.

The construction of Caribbean identity in Britain

It is something of a paradox that it is in Britain that people from the Commonwealth or English-speaking Caribbean have developed the strongest sense of a collective Caribbean identity.[1] It would appear that at the main destination of Caribbean migrants, the USA, there is a far stronger sense of individual island identities than of a regional Caribbean or even West Indian identity.[2] There may be several factors at work here. For example, the historically longer tradition of English-speaking Caribbeans migrating to the USA and forming their own distinctive communities is one factor. Another may be the strong tendency for all arriving groups to take advantage of the American physical and social space to form their own entities, and mix only intermittently with others at points of work and the selling and purchasing of commodities. And there is also the fact that the points of departures (or 'the islands', as some Americans refer to the Caribbean) and the points of arrival on the continent are close enough to encourage frequent visits and the renewal of ties with home. While more familiar in terms of educational systems, language, political systems, and so many other shared factors, John Bull's islands are more distant, and with the end of empire they have more closely embraced a European destiny. In contrast, Uncle Sam has paid closer attention to his 'sphere' or 'backyard' in the region, particularly after the Cuban Revolution of 1958 and the missile crisis of the early 1960s.

However, the stronger sense of a collective regional Caribbean identity in Britain must partly be understood within the context of the dispersed nature of the Caribbean itself. After all, within the region there are several Caribbeans (French, Spanish, Danish, American and Dutch), each reflecting the diverse histories of European conquest and settlement, different patterns of African chattel slavery, Indian, Chinese and

European indentureship. To this list must be added the rivalries and conflicts between different European powers from the sixteenth to the nineteenth centuries, and from the 1890s the powerful appearance of Uncle Sam in all the subregions established by Europe. These interventions in the configuration of the region have left their lasting marks on the Caribbean as well as on the many people who have migrated across the Atlantic, particularly to Britain, France and the Netherlands.

Of particular relevance in this large regional picture is the fact that the Commonwealth Caribbean strongly reflects not only the mercantilist economic but also the military, particularly the naval, interests of imperial Britain at the end of the Napoleonic Wars in 1815. The English-speaking islands are scattered across the region, with Spanish and French-speaking islands interspersed between them. This absence of territorial contiguity meant that there were relatively few points of contact between the people of these islands within the region. In the East Caribbean, islands such as Trinidad, Barbados and St Lucia are physically close and therefore enjoyed relatively strong links with each other. On the other hand, Jamaicans (some 800 miles to the north-west of Barbados) had little opportunity to interact with other English speakers in the region. The elites apart, the opportunities for ordinary English-speaking Caribbeans to meet each other in the region came through the experience of migration to the then British Honduras (now Belize), at the building of the Panama Canal on the isthmus in the 1880s, and in Cuba on the sugar plantations as a result of sugar demands in war-torn Europe after 1914.

These general remarks are relevant because it must be borne in mind that Jamaicans constituted a simple majority of people who migrated from the region to Britain. While being physically close to Cuba (Spanish-speaking) and Haiti (French and Creole-speaking), Jamaicans and other English-speaking Caribbeans arriving in Britain after the docking of SS *Empire Windrush* at Tilbury in 1948 would have been fairly ignorant about each other. The isolation of Jamaica from the rest of the subregion was a key factor in 1962 that enabled the deeply conservative Jamaica Labour Party to persuade voters to leave the West Indian Federation that had been formed in 1958. It is still the case that in ordinary conversations some people in Jamaica will refer to other West Indians as 'small island people', and this was certainly how Jamaicans referred to their co-regionalists during the period of migration and settlement in Britain from the late 1940s to the 1960s. This can have its own comic ironies: some folks from islands smaller than Jamaica can be heard referring to others as being 'small islanders', and Guyana which is located on the South American continent and is physically 20 times the size of Jamaica, is also regarded as a 'small island', because of her small population. The phrase is not merely about physical size; it conveys the sense that big denotes progress, participation in the events of the wider world, and the opposite of backwardness and unsophistication. But some attitudes about each other portray the 'small islanders' in an advantageous position in relation to Jamaicans. For example, there is a Barbadian perception that Jamaicans are rough and ready folks wont to take offence, ill-educated, do not speak good English, etc. In short, it must be clearly understood that people from the various islands did not share a clear sense of national identity, but rather had a variety of identities as Barbadians, Trinidadians, Jamaicans, St Lucians, and had uninformed though non-antagonistic views about each other.

This is not to say that they were entirely lacking in some sense of shared identity. In the first place, they had crafted the English language for their distinct needs and usage, as strongly reflected in the emergence of a powerful literary tradition coinciding with the migration wave to Britain.[3] An example here is that of the three recent Nobel laureates from the region who have all come from the English-speaking ('small') islands. While Arthur Lewis was honoured for contributions to economics, significantly Derek Walcott and V. S. Naipaul were awarded for contributions to poetry and the novel respectively, and there is a strong cohort of equally outstanding novelists and poets who may yet be honoured by that institution. In the same period, the regional University of the West Indies was established, bringing students together from across this cultural region, and together with the golden period of West Indian cricket from the late 1950s to the late 1980s, came to reflect the emergence of West Indian nationalist aspirations. The emergence of trade unions and political parties, the assertion of semi-professional bodies, and the overall assertion of national independence and nation-building in the region, spawned the birth and the recognition of a diverse West Indian personality, drawing on a range of racial and ethnic heritage. Even so, the islands and Guyana and Belize have remained separate political entities, each, like the ancient Greek city states, very jealous of their apparent sovereignty in the comity of nations.

To varying degrees, some of these complicated observations could be made about the other Caribbeans. With regard to the Dutch and Danish Caribbeans, it may be generally said that they very much resemble the profile of the Commonwealth Caribbean. For example, the Netherlands Caribbean have a presence in the islands as well as on mainland South America, enjoy independence, and have access and continuing links to the European Netherlands. The French experience in the region is at once more dramatic and varied. For example, the main possession in the region, Haiti, has the distinction to have been the site of the only recorded successful slave rebellion in history: Haiti's history is an integral part and parcel of the history of Revolutionary and Napoleonic France in the late eighteenth and early nineteenth centuries. Under Toussaint L'Ouverture and his immediate successors, slaves defeated France in their attempt to continue slavery in the Americas and to use Haiti as the staging post for a major presence on the North American continent. Napoleon's defeat in Haiti led to his need in 1807 to sell the vast Louisiana Territory to Thomas Jefferson, the third and expansionist president of the newly formed USA. Until today, Haiti has had a problematic relationship with France, and reparations are now a major issue on the agenda between the two countries.

With respect to France's other territories in the region (particularly Guadeloupe and Martinique), the relationship has been far more firm than between Britain and the Commonwealth Caribbean. Essentially, these territories have introduced or represent a unique feature in international relations: they are integral parts of the territories of France (along with Reunion, in the Indian Ocean). As overseas departments of France, they enjoy the same rights, have the same responsibilities, etc., as citizens in European continental France. These features give primacy to the question of how Caribbeans are integrated into European France, but this is not the purpose of this chapter. Nor is it the concern of this chapter to explore how people in the region (like people from Mauritius in the Indian Ocean) with both French and British heritages negotiate their integration into metropolitan European nation states and societies. Sufficient are the complexities of people of the English-speaking Caribbean for this discussion. Their condition forced them to construct or invent a collective identity in the circumstances of twentieth-century Britain. In doing so, they picked up on some characteristics of their histories and omitted other aspects; this was not entirely an act of free choice, but partly determined by the context in which they found themselves, particularly with regard to racism, the meeting of other new minorities (most of whom appeared to have been already furnished with a collective identity), and the international situation. Each of these points can briefly be elaborated here.

First, while people from the region were depicted as 'West Indians', by the late 1960s they were becoming 'blacks'. The idea of a 'West Indian' identity was originally that of people from the British Isles who, from the seventeenth century, had settled in the Caribbean or who made their vast wealth from West Indian sugar plantations and African slavery across the Atlantic. The 'West India' interest in eighteenth-century England, for example, counted many 'West Indians' who never even visited the region, but simply enjoyed the profits from their plantations. Thus, the visit of one of these men occasioned Matthew 'Monk' Lewis's great diary of 'a West Indian' planter's tour of his estates in Jamaica, and like his Gothic novel *The Monk*, has become a classic. That age is also represented in nineteenth-century literature such as Jane Austen's work and in the works of generations of twentieth-century West Indian novelists such as Jean Reese, V. S. Naipaul, Wilson Harris and Orlando Patterson.

The change in identity nomenclature from 'West Indians' to 'blacks' to 'African Caribbeans' reflected several events in the decades of the 1960s and the 1970s. These included migration from the Indian subcontinent of people more generally described as Indians, making the term 'West Indian' rather confusing the more Britain moved away from imperial categories. After all, the Caribbeans who came to Britain in significant numbers were predominantly of African heritage, and bore little resemblance to people from South Asia or to the equally misidentified 'Amerindians' (the indigenous populations of the region). Here was a case of the compounding of Christopher Columbus's mistake: the West Indies had come into existence because the great explorer thought he had arrived in the western parts of India (his original destination, via the western route, to bypass the newly established Mediterranean and European power of the Ottomans who after Sultan Mehmet's successful storming of Constantinople in 1553 blocked the land and historic routes to the riches of the East).

Moreover, the two parts of the world which threw up images of cultural and racial assertions in the decades from 1950 to 1970, were the USA where the civil rights movement was ablaze, and Africa, where the process of independence was unfolding. In these circumstances, skin colour as a signifier of racial identity, and Africa as a signifier of broken or shattered historical heritage requiring repair became rallying points in the construction of an identity in the British situation. After all, the racist reception (rejection, discrimination, exclusion) experienced by West Indians who to varying degrees believed that they were coming to the 'mother country', soon disabused them of who they thought they were before their arrival. These West Indians were, as the title of Sheila Patterson's book pointed out, 'dark strangers', skilled workers or more generally rural smallholders; they were not planters nor heiresses and widows with a West Indian fortune to flaunt in the exclusive clubs of metropolitan London and the spa towns reminiscent of the Roman occupation and proud Albion. The picture became immensely more complicated with the presence of Africans directly from Africa, with whom only a distant (though highly inspirational) historical past and skin colour were shared. Even their often presumed common colonial experiences were significantly different, and the slavery past sometimes stood in the way of mutual understanding.

Those West Indians who could not make a purchase on an African past or be linked by colour to African America, had also to construct identities for themselves. Hence, some people of South Asian backgrounds, mainly from Trinidad and Guyana, were excluded from the construction of the new identity of 'African Caribbean' or 'blacks'. In general, people of other backgrounds from the region (Chinese, Europeans, Middle Easterners, etc.) have gone on to exist in a number of social indices with regard to identity. Individuals with these backgrounds have variously distanced or associated themselves with the category of 'Caribbean' people in Britain. This has meant that at any domestic, social or political gathering of West Indians or Caribbeans the racial and cultural mosaic thrown up by this kaleidoscope that is a major feature of the region is always revealed in complex but not conflictual ways. This mosaic has been enriched by accrual of family and kinship links with the majority historic society.

But the changing nomenclature and the mixed texture of the identities of people with backgrounds in that region, suggest a kind of uncertainty about identity, and this generally informs all aspects of social life of Caribbeans in Britain. This uncertainty has many manifestations. For example, notions of beauty vary from pride about being African and being black to the opposites of denying their natural physical attributes (hair length and texture; skin colour, etc.) of these heritages, while maintaining customs regarding beliefs, cuisine, etc., sometimes to the detriment of their health and well-being. Following the cultural revolution expressed in the motto 'black is beautiful' in the 1970s, these developments from the 1980s raise questions about African and Caribbean identities in Britain and the West generally that would have startled Franz Fanon,[4] the Martiniquean French psychiatrist, cultural commentator and philosopher, who was deeply concerned about these aspects of Caribbean integration, which he would most likely have mistakenly seen in one-dimensional terms as a one-way (white-way) process.

The contested or conflicting domain of cultural identity for Caribbeans in Britain proved to be an imponderable social fact for a generation of British social analysts, and they entirely failed to understand the situation.[5] Recent comments on this failure of British social studies make it unnecessary to repeat all the relevant points here.[6] Suffice to say that people in Britain who have come from the Caribbean pose interesting and sometimes uncomfortable questions about their identities for themselves, for other new minority ethnic and/or racial groups, as well as the historic indigenous majority to whom Caribbeans come closest in terms of values, customs and general culture. One of the most intriguing of these questions or problems is the multifaceted problem of how Caribbeans have participated in or integrated into the sociopolitical order of post-imperial Britain.

Caribbean sociopolitical integration

The sociopolitical aspects of participation as an indication of integration are stressed because it has become a truism in academic and popular discourses to say that Caribbeans have not made a distinctive mark in the ownership of economic capital in the country. It may be suggested that this truism now needs a critical revisit, because over time a truism can cease to represent practical social situations. Whatever the actual empirical situation may be with regard to ownership, access and control over material or economic resources by people of Caribbean backgrounds in Britain, it cannot be denied that their presence reveals a profound integration into the social and political systems, with benefits to the commonweal. But the inclusivist or embracing nature of how they have negotiated their integration is highly problematic in a society increasingly being fractured by particularistic and exclusivist forms of identities. I want to reiterate my observation that the problem for Caribbeans in Britain is not so much one of integration as perhaps a problem of being so deeply integrated that the headland of integration has been passed to the point of absorption. But this assertion can be moderated to suggest that this absorption has a two-way flow between Caribbeans and other communities, in the main the historic majority but also with others. Some illustrations of this point are in order here.

First, there is the fact of cultural proximity to the majority indigenous population, and this obscures subtle or nuanced differences as well as significant overlaps. As noted earlier, the various subregions or cultural domains of the Caribbean link different parts to nation states and historical cultural collectivities in Europe: British, Danish, Dutch, French and Spanish. The identities of these European communal entities or collectivities have conditioned the construction of identities within the region, and each subsection of the region has close cultural links with their European counterpart. In terms of language, religion, myths, customs and traditions, each bloc shares close affinity, as reflected in literature, music, visual arts and so forth. Cultural proximity between Caribbeans and populations in West Europe is therefore grounded in religion, language, sports, popular culture, etc., to which Caribbeans have made contributions in their new region of settlements. In Britain, as in the Netherlands and France, athletics and football are highly visible sites exhibiting the participation of Caribbeans in national popular life. In Britain, this is also borne out in popular music, the creation of new phrases in the daily use of language and so forth.

In other words, the general value system accords with that of the majority historic population, as well as with pockets in some of the other new minorities. For example, the post-Reformation pluralism embedded within Protestantism from which, in turn, political tolerance of difference has sprung, is taken for granted as a public value among Caribbean as with indigenous majority British communities. These factors make it difficult unequivocally to describe Caribbean integration into the main body of British society as being either at the end of absorption or integration: integration being taken to mean a contribution from each culture that meet in a common sphere, and absorption being taken to denote the abandonment of one culture for another or where the one culture is able to ingest another and claim elements as part of its own original component. Of course, the relationships between Caribbean and British cultures call for more detailed empirical treatment than can be given here. But the general point is that there is an intricate intertwining that is difficult precisely to disentangle, with regard to what happens when different cultures come to share the same social and physical terrain. These factors make it difficult confidently to assert observations about Caribbean entry, settlement and consolidation into British society. There have been elements of both integration and absorption into the elements that are making the blocks of post-imperial British society.

From this perspective, it may be noted that Caribbeans have been instrumental in introducing (alongside other minorities) a range of colours to popular life in such areas as dress, hairstyles and cuisine. But if the prize for the major contribution to enriching British cuisine must go to South Asian and Chinese entrepreneurs, then undoubtedly Caribbeans can stake a claim to the enrichment of popular life. There may be more than one aspect to this, but crucially the annual Notting Hill Carnival has been the outstanding event, which comes at the end of August and coincides with the last annual public holiday in the country before the celebrations of Christmas in December. Deeply embedded in Catholic traditions, the celebration of Carnival was taken up in Trinidad by slaves and later free people, and has become a hall-mark of that country's heritage that is being imitated in other parts of the Caribbean region. Trinidadians settled in the drab and gloomy streets of Notting Hill, under the leadership of the dynamic Claudia Jones and others organised the street events in much the same way as they would have done in Port of Spain, the capital of Trinidad. But Caribbean London street life was not exclusively Trinidadian. Indeed, as indicated, Jamaicans constituted the majority Caribbean population, and soon the Notting Hill Carnival came to represent the Caribbean as a whole, with Jamaicans playing a major role in the construction of an identity two or more decades ahead of the Caribbean countries. Like West Indian cricket, the English language and literature, and the regional University of the West Indies, the Notting Hill Carnival has become a major pole around which many Caribbeans rally. But not only has it rallied Caribbeans; the Carnival events have been opened to members of all other communities, and their active participation has now come to characterise Carnival as a London calendar event.

Additionally, values and norms are revived, refreshed and trans-formed within the broad British tradition of tolerance and respect for difference; similarly, the Enlightenment's stress on the exercise of reason as the basis of judgement about social action is common not only at the British destination, but also at the points of departure in the Caribbean. Today we are becoming more critically aware of how Europe has influenced the world in recent times, but it is almost generally for-gotten or not widely known that one of the first parts of the world to have been so influenced was the Caribbean. Indeed, it is nearly always forgotten in British discourses that the region cannot be spoken of in the same breath as many do about Africa and Asia: societies in these parts of the world were as old and generally older than many societies in Europe, whereas in the Caribbean post-Columbian social formations commenced largely on a *tabula rasa*. Nearly all indigenous peoples were killed or died during conquest and settlement, and the present popula-tions largely came from Africa, Europe and Asia, with new institutions, customs and traditions.

In the case of the Commonwealth Caribbean, Braithwaite's[7] notion that these were societies differentiated by social stratification rather than social and cultural pluralism as M. G. Smith argued,[8] is persuasive. Braithwaite's hypothesis went on to assert that while each group in Trinidad (Africans, South Asians, Chinese, French, Portuguese, British and others) displayed different customs, traditions and so forth, they nonetheless all shared in imitating or upholding British values. It may be suggested that while in the main this was so, the different groups also brought to bear their own sense of value, traditions and customs in these societies and to one degree or another different parts came to be defining elements in what may now be regarded as Commonwealth Caribbean cultural identities. In Britain itself, different islands have had their impacts on the construction of what appears to be on the cusp of becoming post-imperial British culture and identity. For example, in a very general way it could be said that street culture represented by Carnival has come from Trinidad, but is no longer Trinidadian. In the same way, the music from Kingston, Jamaica, has long defined dimensions of popular British culture, as has use of language, but with nuances that are particularly British. For example, with regard to language, in the advertisement for a Beatles show on television at Christmas 2006, the writer expressed the point that the band 'mash-upped' the situation in which they were appearing. The only deviation from 'good' Jamaican Creole here is to make the phrase adhere to the rule of tenses.

Second, Caribbean communities in Britain have displayed values that perhaps had antecedents in Europe but are more fully developed in Caribbean communities. An example may help to clarify the point: this is the existence of loose or soft boundaries between groups of people. Paradoxically, this followed two centuries of chattel slavery and colonialism, both of which instituted rigid social and political separation along lines of perceived superior and inferior racial and ethnic identities as determined by a white elite who controlled economic, social and political power. The emergence of what historians call 'Creole' society in the Caribbean from the period of slavery,[9] has involved the mixing of people from nearly all regions of the world, and this background has clearly influenced the willingness of Caribbeans in Britain not to counter the natural, human, process of interracial and interethnic social relationships.

Consequently, there is perhaps no other new minority group in British society which is more socially intertwined with the indigenous population, particularly at the broad base of the British social (class) pyramid. This social characteristic is reflected and reinforced by the sharing and intertwining of popular culture (sports, music, visual and performing arts, colloquial speech, etc.) to such an extent that it is sometimes hardly noticeable what is the Caribbean influence and which the majority population's. The process of raciation in the Caribbean (that process whereby peoples from various parts of the world with different racial identities had an opportunity by accident of being within the first wave of early capitalist formation to meet, mingle and mix) is not, of course, unique in human relationships. It could be hypothesised, however, that in recent centuries this process has been more pronounced in the Caribbean than in other places.

It may be suggested that the ready willingness to cross boundaries or to refuse to allow racial and ethnic differences to become fixed barriers can be explained by reference to two relevant characteristics that are essential to an understanding of Caribbean cultures. First, there is the strong sense of individual worth, and second, there is its complementary sense of equality of all individuals. In brief, whatever aspects of social life in Caribbean communities and families we care to observe, we see evidence of the same phenomenon, namely the individual acting in their own chosen interest. This strong sense of individual autonomy has become a major aspect of Caribbean societies in the region and in communities in Britain. In general, it is assumed that the emphasis on self-autonomy is a product of postmodernity, but with regard to Caribbeans this trait came much earlier as part of modernity itself, and has since been reinforced by the widely shared experience of migration from the nineteenth century to the present.

One example of the exercise of autonomy is the tendency for organisations to fragment along ideological lines proffered by strong, articulate and enterprising individuals who attract followers, who in turn soon question their leaders, and continue the process of formation–break–formation of groups. This perspective of social life has powerfully influenced several aspects of community action, to the chagrin of local elected leaders in British cities. The simultaneously low participation of Caribbeans in voting at national elections coupled with high awareness of public issues is another case in point. Concomitantly, much the same trend has been observed in the majority indigenous electorate, and particularly since the 2005 elections has become a major concern for the political parties.

But perhaps a clearer example of a convergence of general British and Caribbean life is to be found in the changing living arrangements that are emerging. For the better part of the nineteenth and twentieth centuries, families in Britain could generally be described as nuclear, characterised by consensual marriage between a man and a woman sharing a common domicile, followed by the births of children, a commitment to the welfare of all members of the family within the same household or commonly shared space. Just as in the workforce we cannot any longer take for granted a career or occupation for the totality of our working lives, so too it is becoming the case that families no longer necessarily share the characteristics mentioned here. Consequently, the institution of the family now exhibits a variety of forms or patterns. I have therefore tried to use the phrase 'living arrangements' that people construct rather than the more constraining concept of 'the family', or alternatively, use the plural 'families' in discussions about what we once confidently called the family. But the changing nature of families can be disturbing because it brings onto the public, policy and moral agenda new and perplexing problems. While the change brings greater choice, tolerance and freedom they are accompanied by alienation, isolation, neglect and suffering for members of the institution we call the family, and for individuals.

The peaks and troughs brought about by these changes in living arrangements have been experienced by Caribbean families. In this respect the maternal-orientated, single-parent, lone-mother household, resulting in the fracturing of the nuclear family type that is presently occurring in Britain, has long been characteristic of Caribbean living arrangements. In majority British society it is becoming acceptable for adults to have more than one long-lasting sexual partner, children with more than one of these partners, and to have children before taking the marriage vows. These practices varied according to class and colour; they were more common at the base of the social pyramid occupied by the black population, although they were introduced by the white male population from the days of slavery.[10] Such practices increase the complexity of family structures or forms. For example, as in the Caribbean, families are now increasingly having a number of siblings who are parented by stepmothers and stepfathers, and perhaps in these circumstances the extended kinship network is becoming more important in the socialisation of the young, with grandparents re-entering the family scene as crucial players in family maintenance. My point here is that these features of the modern British family have long been characteristics of Caribbean families, and in this respect these practices have been precursors to what is now becoming more common and socially acceptable.

Additionally, I have suggested elsewhere that Caribbean sociopolitical integration into British society has been characterised by an absence of any particularistic demands on society.[11] Demands that Caribbeans made in negotiating their way into British society have been of a universal kind, that is, their demands appeal across all communities and tend to lead to the improvement of important aspects of society. In other words, while Caribbeans were at the forefront of making demands on British society from the late 1950s to the late 1980s, at no point did they frame these in ways that resulted in benefits exclusively for themselves. For example, in 1981 confrontations with an unnecessarily over-policing authority in Brixton led to the Scarman Report,[12] and the murder of Stephen Lawrence led to the McPherson Report,[13] raising issues about policing, accountability and communities as a whole. In the field of education, perhaps the single most troubled area of life for Caribbeans in Britain, the concerns of parents about the education their children were receiving in the 1970s and into the early 1980s led to the Rampton Report[14] and the Swann Report (1985).[15] These reports were not confined to Caribbeans but took on board the national situation, and their statements about diversity and the way forward were relevant to the nation as a whole. They raised issues about fairness and equality in the future construction of British society.

Of course, it could be argued that the universality of the demands of Caribbeans in British society follows logically from their history and the cultural baggage with which they came to Britain. This may be expressed another way: it is not possible for Caribbeans to make particularistic demands, because culturally their problems and needs are best mobilised by bringing on board a democratic majority with whom there are human links that transcend ethnic and racial boundaries. In the circumstances, it is as well that this is so in the British case, because Caribbeans are everywhere a minority, and could never hope on their own democratically to win in any given conflict of interests. Their practice suggests that they realise that they can win only through persuasion and sharing, not total opposition to, or disregard for, the interests of others. They have been able to have their voices heard, not as a group so much as individuals asserting demands that build on what is already established within the majority society, but which requires reasserting, sharpening and to become more widely applicable. This generalised perspective has been embraced even when Caribbean people have been rejected, so that the biblical statement that 'the stone that the builders refused, has become the head cornerstone' is not only popular in the songs of Bob Marley, but also as a signifier of what has been brought to the making of post-imperial British society.

The problem of Caribbeans' integration into British society

These remarks suggest that there is a fundamental contradiction in the format or design of Caribbean integration into British society. On the one hand, as argued so far, there is a close proximity between the cultures of Caribbeans and the majority historic population, and from this perspective Caribbeans may be regarded as being well integrated into the general culture (language, religion, leisure and sporting activities, political life, work and so forth). Caribbean families in Britain are also interlinked with Africans, Chinese and South Asians through social encounters and engagements in the Caribbean. On the other hand, perhaps the single most frequent experience that Caribbean people have consistently pointed to as significant in their lives as individuals and as communities, has been racism, that is, discrimination on the basis of colour (race). It is as if the very fact of proximity impels an urge to create distance, but the frequency and longevity of 'meeting, mixing, and combining' (to modify a phrase from the social and cultural pluralist theorists) have meant that social practices have intertwined to an extent that it is a difficult matter to separate mainstream or majority cultural factors from those associated with Caribbeans. Consequently, we have to ask whether there is a case of cultural absorption or integration, and if so, in what direction this process is going. There are some complex and interesting characteristics to this conundrum which should be disentangled.

First, while having the formal political and cultural rights as members of the British nations, Caribbeans experienced discrimination in some key areas of national life, and this placed limits on the degree or extent of their integration. This has been well documented over the decades in the various Policy Studies Institute's surveys from Daniel's work,[16] to Modood et al.,[17] in the public reports mentioned earlier, and a sizeable body of academic research depicting British racism. But, as suggested, the struggles of Caribbeans against discrimination in such areas as the law, housing, education, employment and so forth, have been fought on the basis of the country's own long-established methods of opposition to injustice going back to Magna Carta in the thirteenth century, and drawing upon the Abolitionist, Chartist and Suffragette movements in subsequent centuries. Such action includes public demonstrations, oppositional protests, forging links with other minorities as well as elements within the majority population who share similar values, and accompanied by a raft of publications in the attempt to persuade.

A second and perhaps more problematic example of overcoming discrimination or exclusion has been the emergence and development of the black-led churches. Rejection or refusal to have Caribbean Anglicans, Catholics, Methodists and so forth in the historic denominations, forced Caribbeans to found their own places of worship, without excluding others. The result is that integration has not occurred evenly within the Christian communities, as might have been expected. Instead, there has been a widening of the space for different communities to practise their Christian beliefs. Religion is an important aspect of Caribbean identities, but integration has taken the form of a parallel development, though without any major conflict.

A similar picture is evident in many other areas of social life. For example, the vast majority of Caribbeans have been integrated into the working classes as defined by occupation, education and residence. This is not surprising, because this may be so for most groups at the point of entry, particularly with regard to initial occupation and residence. However, many migrants achieve upward social mobility for their offspring, or the offspring do so for themselves over a generation or two. What appears to be distinctive about Caribbean integration is that the process has been characterised more by a downward than by an upward social mobility. To be sure, there are individuals and pockets here and there who have integrated into the middle classes (the professions, public services, etc.), but they do so as individuals and they tend to be bereft of middle-class networks for help and support. Such persons depend on their individual worth, their immediate friendship networks, and their immediate family members. Consequently, there is little or no notion of a Caribbean middle class providing leadership within 'communities' to which they unambiguously belong; it is not surprising that almost invariably Caribbean intellectuals and spokespersons dismiss this notion with scepticism. Increasing occupational and residential choice inhibits development of sizeable exclusive Caribbean neighbourhoods consisting of all social classes. Consequently, those who seek to provide an element of community leadership tend to do so around an agenda of memories of past sufferings and achievements, myths of communal solidarity, and state support for specific local initiatives around felt needs. And yet, there is any number of Caribbean public figures in various areas of national life. However, the point is that they are not community leaders, but public figures who have made their way as individuals in a competitive market.

A very problematic aspect of the integration of Caribbeans has been their very response to discrimination which may be leading to further structural exclusion in some areas of national life. Education will suffice as an example. It cannot be overstressed how important Caribbean immigrant parents regarded the acquisition of education for their children from the point of entry in the 1950s to the period of settlement in the 1970s, and consolidation thereafter. But there was much misunderstanding on their part about the workings of the British educational system. It is still so today. In those early decades, parents carried over from the Caribbean the view that the school and the teacher had the interest of the child in mind, and that as parents they could leave their children entirely in the hands of the school. After all, these children were attending secondary schools; and in the Caribbean secondary school meant a grammar school education, not what Alistair Campbell famously described as the 'bog standard' education that modern and some comprehensive schools provided in cities up and down the country for the working classes. In the Caribbean education was, along with the clergy, a major avenue for upward social mobility, and this was part of the migrants' dream for their children.

Both Caribbean parents and the academic literature have tended to place the responsibility for the poor performance of Caribbean boys in British schools on the school and the teacher. But this is only part of the story. The failure of the schools to meet parental aspirations was not entirely the fault of the teachers; it was perhaps more a matter of the distance between expectations of Caribbean parents and the understanding that British teachers had of their tasks. Coming from a school system still steeped in the Victorian and Edwardian notion of schooling (with strict discipline, and mode of teaching and learning, specific targets, etc.) the parent thought the teacher and the school held the child's interest to be paramount, while the teacher may have had career prospects or the public image of the school uppermost on a list of priorities. This is not to say, however, that there were no dedicated, diligent teachers. Indeed, individual Caribbean children who were educationally successful in the schools during those decades owe a great deal to such dedicated teachers and not only to chance. But there is little doubt that parents, teachers and schools had mismatched expectations of the school system.

This mismatch has continued well into present times. There is anecdotal evidence, for example, to suggest that while there are individual families of Caribbean background who could pay for their children to receive a private education, there is a reluctance to do so. There appears to be a belief that to do so is to betray loyalty to working-class values and virtues, as well as left-wing or progressive social and political views. On the other hand, there are parents who have been comfortable about sending their children to the Caribbean to receive such education. These seemingly contradictory attitudes spring from perceptions of acceptable class behaviour in Britain, which do not apply in the Caribbean. After all, it would appear that the majority of Caribbean middle-class members have gained their upward social mobility in the public arena on a left-wing platform. They cannot, therefore, be seen to want to advance their children through private or grammar school education. This would be to betray class solidarity. Consequently, financial resources tend not to go into educational investment for the next generation as appears to be case in some other groups, but into consumption of popular cultural artefacts. While this itself feeds into much cultural creativity, it perhaps also over-represents Caribbeans in these areas of general social life, and creates a cultural perspective that privileges and honours almost exclusively sports people, popular musicians and DJs, who become dominant models to emulate. In themselves, these aspirations are lofty and meaningful, but they are also representing exceptional abilities and achievements, not the more realisable goals of most individuals in society. The blissful unawareness of the distance of this world of dreams from the mainstream of the society in which they live, may again be creating recipes for continuing failures and new frustrations in their lives and for future generations.

The mismatch of expectations and reality has taken a new turn from the 1990s. This is the integration of Caribbeans in the post-1992 mass higher education system. There is a tendency for young Caribbeans to seize the opportunity for higher education, but in their own localities. Thus, they continue to live at home and in their neighbourhoods, and do not expose themselves to the challenges of the wider world. Some tend to feel sheltered and comfortable, but they do not come to acquire several of the basic social skills required for successful competition in the wider world. Consequently, when failure to successfully compete in the labour market ensues, racism is likely to be offered as the explanation. In particular, some young men fail on nearly all social and educational indices because they develop and proudly exhibit antisocial and threatening attitudes, such as the refusal to communicate verbally, display an inability to be polite to others, and in claiming 'respect' for themselves are often arrogantly neglectful of according 'the other' person the same rights. Many young women appear to learn from early on that 'bad' behaviour in public will gain them 'kudos' or 'respect' among their peers and this is carried into the classroom as acceptable behaviour that accords with one perception of the majority public culture. There appears to be confusion over modes of protest and modes of ordinary social behaviour, and the irony here is that responsible persons dare not intervene to suggest acceptable ways of social encounters and exchange. Something called 'coolness' becomes a norm and neither their families nor the schools seem able to undertake the necessary task of infusing norms more appropriate for engaging with others.

This point is deliberately stressed in order to emphasise that these aspects of culture are also aspects of integration. At a wider societal level, Caribbean integration into British society has massively taken on board the culture of the celebrity whose behaviour is always tolerated even if not acceptable. For example, through the media, business enterprises, politicians, and more recently leading churchmen tend to endorse if not promote the badly behaved, almost antisocial, sportsman, musician, entertainer, and antisocial young people. Many of these figures enjoy publicity, notoriety, a wealthy lifestyle, and sometimes apparent instant success. The culture of instant gratification appears to be there for the taking, and this is coupled with the sense that individuals can make their own decisions, live by them and chart their own selfish ways through life. If there are unfortunate consequences, as inevitably there are for some, there is the ever-present welfare state to pick up the tab, and if the state cannot do so because of perhaps more needy demands and the imperative of keeping taxation to affordable levels, then it is often perceived as 'the government's fault'.

The general point here is that, as in several other areas of national life, Caribbeans appear to be at the forefront or in the vanguard of the onslaught on responsible citizenship. We may need to question whether this is the usual media over-representation, and to gauge through empirical research the level of their participation in the promotion of irresponsible citizenship, but in any case these do suggest some of the less desirable aspects of Caribbean integration into British society. This is not sociologically abnormal. To one degree or another some of these negatives are true for all communities, but such is the nature of communities (there are positive as well as disconcerting aspects), and as social analysts we should strive to understand these beyond the bounds of ideological commitments.

Conclusion

This perspective on Caribbeans in Britain presents several questions about what we might learn about the nature of their integration into British society, and it is suggested that there are at least three important points to be noted from this experience of entry, settlement and consolidation on these shores. First, Caribbeans necessarily challenged and continue to be something of a 'thorn in the flesh' of British society because of their cultural proximity, as well as their racially mixed heritage as reflected in such social factors as names, religion, language, values and norms. Indeed, Caribbeans have a tendency to stress norms such as individuality to a point that anarchists would approve and commend. Second, while all newcomers to a well-established social order undergoing change but not about to atrophy will have urgent demands, it is obviously of immense benefit to them if these demands can be raised in a manner that does not threaten other newcomers nor the indigenous communities. This suggests that leaders or spokespersons in new communities need to find ways of exploring and explaining the points of connections rather than points of division from other groups. Third, at the same time, there needs to be greater awareness that the experience of Caribbeans over the last three or four decades has shown that what, in a time of urgent action (for example the Brixton disturbances), may be seen as an undermining of the social fabric, with time may come to be seen as little more than the demand to be treated equally in the social and political spheres of a changing and therefore healthy society.

Notes

1. See, for example, H. Goulbourne, *Caribbean Transnational Experience* (London and Kingston: Pluto Press and Arawak Publications, 2002).
2. See, for example, N. Foner (ed.), *Islands in the City: West Indian Migration to New York* (Berkeley: University of California Press, 2001).
3. See, for example, A. Walmsley, *The Caribbean Artist Movement, 1966–1972: a Literary and Cultural History* (London: New Beacon Books, 1992).
4. F. Fanon, *Black Skin, White Masks* (London: Macgibbon & Kee, 1968).
5. See, for example, J. Rex and S. Tomlinson, *Colonial Immigrants in a British City: a Class Analysis* (London: Routledge & Kegan Paul, 1979); also G. Dench, *Minorities in the Open Society: Prisoners of Ambivalence* (London: Routledge & Kegan Paul, 1986).
6. H. Goulbourne, 'Families, Communities and Social Capital: Past and Continuing False Prophesies in Social Studies', *Community, Work & Family*, 9/3 (2006).
7. L. Braithwaite, 'Social Stratification in Trinidad: a Preliminary Analysis', *Social & Economic Studies*, 2/2 (1953).
8. M. G. Smith, *The Plural Society in the British West Indies* (California: University of California Press, 1965); also *Culture, Race and Class in the Commonwealth Caribbean* (Kingston: Department of Extra-Mural Studies, University of the West Indies, 1984).
9. See, for example, E. Braithwaite, *The Development of Creole Society in Jamaica 1770–1820* (Oxford: Clarendon Press, 1978).
10. See, for example, R. T. Smith, 'Caribbean Families: Questions of Research and Implications for Policy', in H. Goulbourne and M. Chamberlain (eds),

Caribbean Families in Britain and the Trans Atlantic World (Basingstoke: Palgrave Macmillan, 2001).

11. See, for example, H. Goulbourne, 'A Distrust of Politics?: Participation of People of African Heritage in Britain and the Atlantic World', in W. Berthomière and C. Chivallon (eds), *Diasporas: après quinze années de ferveur* (Pessac: Editions de la Maison des Sciences de l'Homme d'Aquitaine, 2006).

12. Lord Scarman, *The Brixton Disorders, 10–12 April 1981* (London: HMSO, CM 8427, 1982).

13. Sir William McPherson, *The Stephen Lawrence Inquiry* (London: HMSO, CM 4262–1, 1999).

14. A. Rampton, *West Indian Children in our Schools: Interim Report of the Committee of Inquiry into the Education of Children from (sic) Ethnic Groups* (London: HMSO, CM 8273, 1981).

15. Lord Swann, *Education for all: Report of the Committee of Inquiry into Education of Children from Ethnic Minority Groups* (London: HMSO, CM 9453, 1985).

16. W. Daniel, *Racial Discrimination in Britain* (Harmondsworth: Penguin, 1968).

17. T. Modood et al., *Ethnic Minorities in Britain: Diversity and Disadvantage* (London: Policy Studies Institute, 1997).

Select bibliography

Braithwaite, E., *The Development of Creole Society in Jamaica 1770–1820* (Oxford: Clarendon Press, 1978).

Daniel, W., *Racial Discrimination in Britain* (Harmondsworth: Penguin, 1968).

Dench, G., *Minorities in the Open Society: Prisoners of Ambivalence* (London: Routledge & Kegan Paul, 1986).

Fanon, F., *Black Skin, White Masks* (London: Macgibbon & Kee, 1968).

Foner, N. (ed), *Islands in the City: West Indian Migration to New York* (Berkeley: University of California Press, 2001).

Goulbourne, H., *Caribbean Transnational Experience* (London and Kingston: Pluto Press and Arawak Publications, 2002).

Goulbourne, H. and Chamberlain, M. (eds), *Caribbean Families in Britain and the Trans Atlantic World* (Oxford: Palgrave Macmillan, 2001).

McPherson, Sir William, *The Stephen Lawrence Inquiry* (London: HMSO, CM 4262-1, 1999).

Modood, T. et al., *Ethnic Minorities in Britain: Diversity and Disadvantage* (London: Policy Studies Institute, 1997).

Rampton, A., *West Indian Children in our Schools: Interim Report of the Committee of Inquiry into the Education of Children from (sic) Ethnic Groups* (London: HMSO, CM 8273, 1981).

Rex, J. and Tomlinson, S., *Colonial Immigrants in a British City: a Class Analysis* (London: Routledge & Kegan Paul, 1979).

Scarman, Lord Leslie, *The Brixton Disorders, 10–12 April 1981* (London: HMSO, CM 8427, 1982).

Smith, M. G., *The Plural Society in the British West Indies* (California: University of California Press, 1965).

Smith, M. G., *Culture, Race and Class in the Commonwealth Caribbean* (Kingston: Department of Extra-Mural Studies, University of the West Indies, 1984).

Swann, Lord Michael, *Education for all: Report of the Committee of Inquiry into Education of Children from Ethnic Minority Groups* (London: HMSO, CM 9453, 1985).

Walmsley, A., *The Caribbean Artist Movement, 1966–1972: a Literary and Cultural History* (London: New Beacon Books, 1992).

Conclusion

Gino G. Raymond and Tariq Modood

The contributions to this volume have all proved, in their different ways, that minorities are now setting the agenda in Britain, France and elsewhere in multicultural, post-industrial societies, as they have never done before. Whereas in the immediate aftermath of the immigrants arriving in 1950s Britain from the Caribbean, or the post-independence North African migrants arriving to feed the French economic miracle in the 1960s, the question was how quickly they would adapt to the cultural contours of their host society; the question in recent decades has been the extent to which those contours can be remodelled to adapt to the minorities. The arguments deployed by Modood, Kastoryano and Silverman, that for too long governing elites in Europe, and especially France, have operated according to assumptions that ignored the culture-specific processes that shaped them, constitute points in favour of a more flexible interpretation of the identity of national community that has gained greatly in currency and credibility in recent years. As de Wenden underlines in her concise and cogent analysis of France's understanding of its own history, the imperative of national cohesion is, to a significant degree, motivated by the desire to prevent a resurgence of those centripetal forces of language, religion and regional identity that divided the country before the great modernising and centralising project of nation-building that was launched in 1789.

The new factor in the equation, however, is, paradoxically, what in French might be called a *repli identitaire* or defensive form of identification that is marked by its extraterritoriality. While in the past anxiety was caused in the national community by divisive allegiances originating from within it, now we see the operation of allegiances and identifications that are transnational and even global. Michel Wieviorka sounds a timely and cautionary note by suggesting that the evolution of

161

the debate on the recognition and accommodation of identities may take us further away from, rather than closer to, an unambiguous and applicable response, and the concomitant of this is borne out by Nadia Kiwan's research which points to the way young people at the crossroads of cultures may engage in processes of 'subjectivisation' resulting in movement between poles of identification that are in constant tension.

The events of 7/7 in London demonstrated in the most dramatic fashion, as did the mobilisation, national and international, against the new French legislation banning the veil in the public sphere and most notably schools, that globalisation is not a purely economic process but also a cultural one. Pnina Werbner illustrates the unreality of the expectation that cultural and religious practices can be deposited at the frontier of a new host society, and argues anyway that the history of Europe shows that the invisibility of minorities is no guarantee of acceptance or security. The notion that minority communities can operate according to a variety of loyalties at the same time is a well-established one, whether it is the carnival-like transfer of national identity to visiting sports teams established in the UK in the 1970s, especially in the domain of cricket, or the pattern of frequent visits 'home' to North Africa among young French people whose parents or grandparents came from that region, as discovered by Nadia Kiwan. But the developments of the last two decades have given a deeper significance to the notion of competing and/or coterminous identities. The end of the ideological cleavage that characterised the post-war settlement shaping the world for most of the second half of the twentieth century, the global movements of capital and people, the instantaneous and universal access to communication, and the emergence of supranational jurisdictions with the accompanying supranational interpretation of the notion of rights, have dislocated the erstwhile vertical integration of concepts of state, nationhood and citizenship.

As the unitary and statist French Republic has discovered, it is in reality difficult to recognise the right to practise and preserve a minority language, without acknowledging the particularity of the community practising it. This quandary, highlighted by the European Union's endorsement of minority languages, is also symptomatic of a wider issue: the supranational jurisdiction of the EU inevitably recasts the relationship between the individual and the national state. If the jurisdiction of the EU can be superimposed on, and exceed the jurisdiction of, the national state, can the same therefore not occur with regard to the citizen's hierarchy of obligations? For countries like France and Britain, with large populations of immigrant origin, does the process of 'enculturation' have to remain national, when the judicial parameters for its operation, the ultimate means of legal redress, and its possible future foundation constitutionally, are supranational?

The foregoing and troubled problematic that has emerged with regard to the relationship between territory and identity has resulted in a situation where the possibility exists of sustaining the sentiment that neither the departure from a country of origin, nor the arrival in a new host society, are definitive or permanent. Moreover, when this sentiment is underpinned by a transnational value system defining a community that is one based on belief, then an imagined community that knows no frontiers can exercise an exceptional mobilising power that leads, for example, young people in France or Britain whose forebears established themselves in Europe generations ago, to endure the sufferings of the Palestinian people as if it were something occurring in their immediate proximity.

Certain observers have argued, with some justification, that the official recognition given to the Muslim minority in its midst by the French state, through the setting up in 2003 of the Conseil National du Culte Musulman (the French equivalent of the Muslim Council of Great Britain), with the backing of the then Interior Minister, Nicolas Sarkozy, was little more than the institutionalisation that had been offered to other faith groups in France, such as Protestants and Jews. On the other hand, one could suggest that the French state has made a de facto recognition that its Muslim citizens have shared loyalties that can legitimately extend beyond those due to the nation state. The visit by leaders of the Conseil National du Culte Musulman to Iraq in 2004, with the tacit approval of the French government, was both an attempt to make those loyalties weigh in the balance in the endeavour to free French captives there, and a broader opportunity for the French state to repair its image in the world community, especially in Muslim societies, after the furore created by the ban on headscarves in the public sphere.

While holding fundamentally to the inculcation of common values, rather than the formalisation of difference, which is the credo that underpins the 'one and indivisible Republic', French governments have nonetheless shown increasing pragmatism in their attitudes towards minorities. As the state-funded Centre d'Analyse Stratégique underlined in 2006, the past decade and a half in France has seen the rise of challenges to the republican assumption that is was not possible, and certainly not legal, to discriminate between France's citizens in terms of race or religion. The stubborn realities of social discrimination have led to a growing acceptance, even in government circles, that the elaboration of genuinely egalitarian policies cannot succeed if the government refuses to collect statistics that allow it to measure the influence of factors like race and religion on the ability of its citizens to obtain good housing, employment commensurate with their qualifications and enjoy the social mobility that should come with those things.

Few politicians of the mainstream centre-right or left in France would dismiss some of the ideas that have been floated in recent years to help repair what has been described, for many minorities living in the deprived outer suburbs or *banlieues*, as a social elevator stuck in the basement. One of the ideas canvassed as deserving of state backing, therefore, has been the introduction of standardised, anonymous job application forms so that, for example, candidates with Arabic names do not fall at the first hurdle as the victims of prejudice. Another element of positive discrimination that already exists in the public sphere is to be found in selection to those elite educational institutions called the *grandes écoles*. In 2001 the Ecole de Sciences Politiques in Paris launched its *Conventions* with the secondary education sector. These were the fruit of a collaboration with schools in *zones d'éducation prioritaire* (ZEPs), those areas where even the brightest pupils could not be insulated from the effects of the economic and social deprivation characterising those localities where their schools were sited. The objective of the *Conventions* therefore was to provide an alternative route to the classic method of competitive entrance exams, for those students from deprived areas with the potential to succeed at the Ecole de Sciences Politiques.

Ironically, the pragmatism which is traditionally attributed to the attitude of the British state towards its minorities, is what has been leading it on a path of convergence towards its French counterpart. While the French state has defined its opposition to the veil in education from a posture defined by its republican ideology, the British state has been moving towards a position that, in practice, is not dissimilar. In October 2006, Aishah Azmi, a bilingual learning support assistant, lost her appeal at an employment tribunal against dismissal from Headfield Church of England junior school in Dewsbury, for refusing to remove the full veil or *niqab* in the classroom. In a comment with a rather Gallic resonance, the local Labour MP Shahid Malik was at pains to point out the difference between the educational sphere and wider civil society. The issue, he argued, was not about religion, and that while he supported Ms Azmi's right to wear her veil in society, it was not appropriate in the classroom since it could only inhibit her ability to help the children.

On 21 February 2007 a girl aged 12 lost her court battle against the decision by her school in Buckinghamshire to ban the *niqab*. In his judgment Justice Silber argued that the ban was proportionate, given the security implications of not being able to identity individuals on the school premises, and that wearing the *niqab* could jeopardise communication between teacher and pupil. In the days leading up to the judgment, Britain's first Muslim peer, Lord Ahmed of Rotherham, had told the *Yorkshire Post* that he believed the *niqab* to be a mark of separation, segregation and defiance against mainstream British culture. Thus within months of the heavyweight Labour politician Jack Straw's comments in October 2006 that he viewed the *niqab* as a statement of separation, and therefore asked wearers attending his constituency surgeries to remove it, there was a widespread expression of the feeling that the accommodation of difference could not be a one-way process. Legitimate communitarian concerns had too often become 'communalist' ones, quite frequently articulated by self-appointed male leaders.

Both in the campaigns of the various candidates for the presidency of the French Republic in 2007 and in the political manoeuvring prior to the departure of Tony Blair from office, there was the (familiar in France but not so familiar in England) evocation of the responsibilities of the individual citizen, and that citizenship had to be a demonstrably positive choice, as opposed to a passive process. Britain had already instituted its citizenship ceremonies, proposed citizenship tests and some politicians even mooted the idea of a probationary period before citizenship was conferred on an irrevocable basis. Apart from the obvious degree of political self-interest motivating some of these utterances, it was also a tacit admission that there had been some naivety inherent in the British liberal consensus on these issues. As Vincent Latour demonstrates in his investigation of the support for community-based initiatives in Bristol, there was clear naivety at the level of local government in not realising that divisions between minorities might not only be impervious to national policies of community cohesion, but could operate within them to replicate racial and religious divisions, and potential tensions.

In the post 9/11 world it is inevitable that the focus should be on the challenges posed by accommodating certain, newer minorities in France and Britain, rather than the lessons to be learned from the experience of older ones. Implicit in Harry Goulbourne's contribution, however, is the notion that the comfortable coexistence of identities is constructed at the base of the social pyramid, determined by the interaction at the grass roots, and that perhaps the most effective campaigns for the recognition and respect of difference are those predicated on the need to enhance the rights of all.

Index